CONGRESS' PERMANENT MINORITY?

Studies in American Political Institutions and Public Policy
General Editor: James W. Ceaser, University of
Virginia

Congress' Permanent Minority? Republicans in the U.S. House
by William F. Connelly, Jr., and John J. Pitney, Jr.

CONGRESS' PERMANENT MINORITY?

Republicans in the U.S. House

William F. Connelly, Jr.
John J. Pitney, Jr.

ROWMAN & LITTLEFIELD PUBLISHERS, INC.

ROWMAN & LITTLEFIELD PUBLISHERS, INC.

Published in the United States of America
by Rowman & Littlefield Publishers, Inc.
4720 Boston Way, Lanham, Maryland 20706

3 Henrietta Street
London WC2E 8LU, England

Published in a paperback edition
by Littlefield Adams Quality
Paperbacks which is distributed
by National Book Network.
ISBN 0-8226-3032-X (pbk: alk. paper)

British Cataloging in Publication Information Available

Library of Congress Cataloging-in-Publication Data

Connelly, William F., 1951–
Congress' permanent minority? : Republicans in the U.S. House /
William F. Connelly, Jr., John J. Pitney, Jr.
p.   cm.
Includes index.
1. Republican Party (U.S. : 1854–)   2. United States. Congress.
House.   3. United States—Politics and government—1945–1989.
4. United States—Politics and government—1989–   I. Pitney, John
J., 1955– . II. Title.
JK2356.C66   1994   324.2734—dc20   94-531   CIP

ISBN 0-8476-7923-3 (cloth: alk. paper)

Printed in the United States of America

∞ ™ The paper used in this publication meets the minimum requirements of
   American National Standard for Information Sciences—Permanence
   of Paper for Printed Library Materials, ANSI Z39.48—1984.

To Becky and Lisa

Contents

Figures

Tables

Studies in American Political Institutions and Public Policy

General Editor's Foreword

Congress' Permanent Minority? is the inaugural volume in this series, comprised of political science works on contemporary American politics that address the enduring question of how institutions and policies can best function to sustain a healthy liberal democratic government in the United States. This volume, written by two fine young scholars, traces the recent history of the Republican party in the House of Representatives and explores alternative models of the most effective strategy for the minority party. Benefiting from years of direct contact with the House and the Republican party, these authors tell a story of recent developments that will fascinate every close observer of the House. At the same time, they step back from the flow of events to focus on the larger implications of their subject for improving Congress.

James W. Ceaser
Professor of Government and Foreign Relations
The University of Virginia

Acknowledgments

Our gratitude starts with the American Political Science Association's Congressional Fellowship Program, which has flourished under the guidance of Cathy Rudder, Tom Mann, Chris Deering, and Kay Sterling. As Congressional Fellows, we both had the privilege of working for Dick Cheney, and Jack Pitney later worked for Jerry Lewis. Both have been friends and mentors.

Claremont McKenna College and Washington and Lee University have been unstinting in their support. We are also grateful to the APSA and the Dirksen Center. The Governmental Studies program of the Brookings Institution, directed by Tom Mann, hosted Bill Connelly as a guest scholar. We are also indebted to the political scientists and practitioners who have commented on facets of this project: Stan Bach, Bob Biersack, Jerry Climer, Larry Evans, Frank Gregorsky, Paul Herrnson, Tom Hofeller, Charles O. Jones, Phil Kawior, Robin Kolodny, Jeff Nelson, David Nichols, R. J. Pestritto, Jim Pinkerton, Nicol Rae, Howard Reiter, Barbara Sinclair, Steve Smith, and the editor of this series, James W. Ceaser.

Among current and former House Republican staff, we are especially grateful to Bill Pitts, Bill Gavin, Bob Okun, Don Wolfensberger, Brenda Benjamin, Doc Syers, Dave Ramey, Flint Lewis, and Jack Calkins. Finally, special thanks goes to former Congressman Bill Frenzel, whose insight and ready humor provided unfailing balance; and Michael J. Malbin, whose detailed comments greatly improved the final product. We remember two departed friends: Charley Tidmarch and Tim Wyngaard. We also appreciate the assistance of Mary Bobenia, Robert Burger, Chuck Erdman, Ryan Iwasaka, Sharon Lee, Brian Menard, and Shannon Kelly.

Most of all, we are grateful for the loving support, encouragement, and forbearance of our wives, Becky and Lisa. As authors always do, we accept full responsibility for the limitations of this study.

Chapter 1

Introduction

The 1952 election marked the last time Republicans won a majority of seats in the United States House of Representatives. The House GOP thus holds a unique place in congressional history: never has a party dwelt in the minority for even half as long (see Figure 1-1). At the start of the 103d Congress in 1993, none of the House Republicans—and only four of the Democrats—had ever served under a GOP speaker. Like most Americans in the 1990s, the youngest lawmakers had not even been *born* when Republicans last ran the House.[1]

The House GOP's extraordinary situation raises a number of questions:

- Who are the House Republicans, and what do they want?

- What has minority status meant for House Republicans? How has it affected their ability to voice their beliefs and shape public policy?

- How have House Republicans tried to cope with minority status? How has their reaction influenced the workings of Congress?

- What accounts for the House GOP's losing streak? What have political scientists and journalists missed in explaining Democratic control of the House?

- What, if anything, can House Republicans do to win a majority?

- What can scholars learn by studying the House Republicans? Can they find things that they otherwise overlook when they focus only on the majority?

Political scientists have long neglected these questions, particularly the last. Not since 1970, when Charles O. Jones published *The Minority*

1

Figure 1-1
Years of Party Control in the U.S. House

D	1857–1859 ——— 2	
R	1859–1875 ———————————————16	
D	1875–1881 —————— 6	
R	1881–1883 ——— 2	
D	1883–1889 —————— 6	
R	1889–1891 ——— 2	
D	1891–1895 ———— 4	
R	1895–1911 ———————————————16	
D	1911–1919 ————————— 8	
R	1919–1931 ——————————————12	
D	1931–1947 ———————————————16	
R	1947–1949 ——— 2	
D	1949–1953 ———— 4	
R	1953–1955 ——— 2	
D	1955–1995 ————————————————————————— 40	

Party in Congress, have scholars written extensively about the topic.[2] Many political scientists even see House Republicans as unapproachable, or as one colleague put it, "As soon as you find one you can talk to, he gets shot." And indeed, a number of House Republicans do balk at cooperating in academic studies. This reluctance is understandable, though not necessarily justified, because the great majority of political scientists are liberal Democrats.[3]

Whatever its cause, scholarly neglect of a topic tends to feed on itself. Once certain fields of study are well-tilled, researchers flock there to refine or refute previous work.[4] But in doing so, they abandon other fields, which then grow fallow. Because social scientists set their research agendas on the basis of the work of other social scientists, such a field may go untouched for a long time.

This study plows deserted ground, in hopes that others will follow. We seek to learn *about* the House Republicans *from* the House

Republicans, listening to what they say about their unique predicament, weighing their opinions, insights, and disagreements. Much of our material comes from more than 100 interviews with House members and aides, conducted between 1987 and 1992, mostly on a not-for-attribution basis. We also draw on firsthand observations. We both worked as American Political Science Association Congressional Fellows for then-Congressman Dick Cheney (R-Wyoming) during the mid-1980s, while he chaired the House Republican Policy Committee. In addition, one of us (Pitney) has served on the staffs of the House Republican Research Committee and the Republican National Committee.

Why Study the House Republicans?

One reason for taking on this subject is quite plain. Despite the constraints of minority status, Republicans still make up a large part of the House's membership. They can often vex the majority leadership and can sometimes foil it by building coalitions with conservative Democrats. Any description of House politics is incomplete unless it makes room for the GOP.

Likewise, theorists err when they draw sweeping conclusions about legislative life based only on accounts of the majority party. Truisms about House Democrats do not always apply to Republicans, nor would they still apply to the Democrats if they ever lost their majority. Members of the majority think and act differently from members of the minority, so analysts should revise their theories to account for these differences. To distinguish what is common to all lawmakers from what is specific to the majority or minority, political scientists must study both sides.

Expanding the View of Lawmakers' Goals

A careful look at the House Republicans may lead scholars to rethink the linkage between party leadership and lawmakers' goals. According to Richard Fenno, House members want three things: reelection, influence within the House, and good public policy.[5] In recent decades, it has made sense for an individual member of the majority party to want strong party leadership and to work in party activities. Strong majority-party leaders can serve their members' goals in a variety of ways: persuading political action committees

(PACs) to back lawmakers facing tough reelection fights, giving members "a piece of the action" through assignments to committees or party task forces, and making sure that favored legislation gets passed. By laboring faithfully for the party and its leadership, individual members increase their chance of reaping these rewards. There are costs, of course, because strong leaders can induce members to cast votes against their own preferences. If such costs grow too high, members can oust the leadership or curb its power.[6] Since the late 1970s, however, Democrats have continued to support a strong leadership because they have deemed the benefits worth the price.[7]

Things look different from the minority side—something that congressional scholars miss if they only study Democrats. Compared with their majority-party counterparts, leaders of the minority party can do less for the individual members' goals of reelection, influence, and good policy. With little say over the legislative agenda, the minority party has a hard time pushing issue positions or cowing PAC directors. As for influence in the House, members of the minority do not chair legislative committees or subcommittees, so the party can only bestow the less-than-exalted title of "ranking member." Republican Leader Robert Michel (R-Illinois) ruefully observed how constituents react: "Rank? Gee, that smells."[8]

While party involvement provides a House Republican with scant immediate payoff, it carries serious opportunity costs: every hour spent in party activities takes an hour away from answering mail or working on legislation with majority members. Party activity can also have steep direct costs. By fighting a powerful committee chair, a Republican might boost minority morale—while dooming any chance of getting future bills through the committee. By becoming a party spokesperson, a Republican might regularly make the front page of the *New York Times*—while alienating local constituents who see another politician "going Washington." In 1992, Guy Vander Jagt (R-Michigan), head of the National Republican Congressional Committee, lost his seat in a primary election because many voters saw him as a Beltway gamesman who had forgotten his roots.

Conversely, when House Republicans maximize their near-term individual interests, they may be hurting their party. By trading votes with Democrats, they might win pork-barrel projects, advance pet causes, or feel like "players." Such deals undercut party positions and diminish GOP chances of winning a majority. House Republicans would all gain if their party took control, but each can have only a slight impact on the party's majority prospects, which are remote anyway.[9] According to GOP whip Newt Gingrich (R-Georgia):

> There's no question, particularly in the modern era, that it is easier for the minority legislator to accommodate to the system. There are more rewards for being a good minority legislator than there are for trying to become a majority legislator. The system is biased toward putting the minority member to some extent in a courtier relationship to the majority, especially on the committees.

Although political scientists have given little thought to the subject, they should be unsurprised to learn that many House Republicans have succumbed. Putting individual goals ahead of party goals, they have often balked at shoring up their leadership or taking an active role in the life of the party.

What *is* surprising is the extent to which House Republicans *have* kept the party faith. Either as a party or in smaller groups, they have sometimes taken majority-building actions that did not obviously serve their short-term individual interests. In 1989, they chose the highly partisan Gingrich as party whip; and four years later, a majority of House Republicans supported him to be Robert Michel's heir apparent as Republican Leader.

Some House Republicans, at least some of the time, have been motivated by desire to increase their party's strength. Most of them can get reelected if they are careful, but the other satisfactions of congressional life are tainted by the frustrations of minority status. What good is a "seat at the table" if you can never hold the gavel? How much can you really accomplish by attaching a nice small amendment to a big bad bill? In 1986, Henry Waxman (D-California) voiced a common opinion on Capitol Hill: "If we have a united Democratic position, Republicans are irrelevant."[10] This dismissive attitude galls the GOP. Looking back on his twenty-year career, former Representative Bill Frenzel (R-Minnesota) lamented, "the House Republicans feel ignored because they are ignored." "The sense of being in the minority is being left out," said Willis Gradison (R-Ohio), a leading light of the House GOP until his 1993 resignation. "We know when the trains are leaving but the engineer doesn't care whether we're on board or not. It leaves when he's ready."[11] The short-term incentives for acquiescence often override this frustration, but it keeps festering. Ambitious politicians do not fight their way to Washington to become mere cargo.

Looking at Leaders

House Democrats resent the GOP's harsh attacks on the way they run the House. Gingrich described their reaction with words that could only make them angrier: "When you have owned the plantation, the idea that one of your slaves wants to drink out of the same glass is clearly an assault. Seen by the slave, it's simply the fact that it's a hot day."

Through this deliberately provocative language, Gingrich seeks to perturb the Democrats, reckoning that a rattled opponent makes mistakes. More important, by telling his GOP colleagues that the majority looks down on them as "slaves," he tries to deepen their distaste for the status quo and make them hungrier for a majority. Whether or not this approach is praiseworthy, it does suggest a wrinkle to the study of legislative leadership. A common image portrays legislative leaders as mere brokers, who take their followers' wants as they find them, and try to cut deals that make them happier.[12] Leaders such as Gingrich do spend much of their time this way, but they go a step beyond by trying to *change* what their members want. Gingrich speaks the language of revolution, constantly urging Republicans to transform their mindsets and adopt new paradigms. To Congress scholars, Gingrich's efforts should serve as a caution against mechanically relying on economic theories of legislative behavior. According to James Q. Wilson, "whereas economics is based on the assumption that preferences are given, politics must take into account the efforts made to change preferences."[13]

Robert Michel more closely fits the traditional model of legislative leadership. To depict Michel as a broker is not to belittle his stewardship, for he has displayed a shrewd sense of political feasibility. As he explained in a thoughtful 1989 speech:

> Ideological activists believe they know the truth and they don't want to negotiate or compromise or even talk about compromise. But in the House, the ability to strike a wise compromise is an essential part of leadership. Ideological activists don't understand that in the House, as on the battlefield, maneuver can often lead to eventual success where a frontal assault might fail.[14]

Michel and Gingrich also have different orientations toward congressional politics. These differences involve more than cosmetics, because they stem from two conflicting strands of the American political tradition, variously known as conventional versus unconventional, establishment versus populist, and most commonly, insider versus outsider.[15] James Ceaser traces such splits to the debate between the Federalists and the Anti-Federalists, as well as the "court" and "country" parties of Georgian England.[16] The Federalists and their English counterparts worked the back rooms of political and financial power, while their opponents came from the outlands, preferring open debate to quiet dealmaking. Today's "outsiderism" defines itself in opposition to elitism, corruption, and politics as usual.

Michel represents the insider orientation, although after decades in the minority, he might question the label. Gingrich, by contrast, consciously casts himself as an outsider by denouncing the Democrats' abuse of House rules and the electoral process, as well as their ties to labor unions and other special interests. Michel seeks incremental change through institutional politics while Gingrich wants to transcend the minority's institutional constraints by appealing to the public and widening the scope of conflict.[17]

Legislative leaders never act as free agents, for they have limited political resources, and they must address their followers' demands and expectations.[18] Nevertheless, it would be a mistake to argue that individual leaders do not matter. House Republicans believe that Gingrich would take them along different paths than Michel, and that no other "outsider" would lead them with quite the same mix of intellect, media instinct, and aggressiveness. In a way, House Democrats agree. According to one top staffer, many regard Gingrich as "the devil incarnate."

Thinking in Time

In 1983, when Gingrich and a number of his allies formed a group called the Conservative Opportunity Society, he seemed to be a fringe figure among House Republicans. Ten years later, he was poised to become their chief. What happened?

Besides his own persuasive powers, he gained strength from membership changes. More than political scientists generally acknowledge, the House GOP consists of overlapping factions based on region, ideology, generation, and political strategy. Through the elections of the 1980s and early 1990s, the factions that favored Gingrich gained members, while opposing factions shrank.

At the same time, the minority's relationship with the majority turned sour. Where Republicans could once win half a loaf by dealing with Democrats, said some minority members, now they had to settle for crumbs. Barber Conable (R-New York), a moderate who served as ranking minority member on the Ways and Means Committee until his 1984 retirement, went even further. Referring to the crusty Texan chairing the Judiciary Committee, Conable said: "Some House Republicans don't even get crumbs. All you get from Jack Brooks are fang marks." Conable attributed his own retirement in part to his waning influence on Ways and Means. "In the later years, anything I got was by the grace of Danny [Rostenkowski]." And according to another former member:

> [At one time] you were looked upon by your colleagues on the other side of the aisle as first, a member of the House, second, as the member from [your state], and third, as a Republican. And that order has been reversed. Now the defining characteristic that labels everybody initially is party. If a member is a Republican, they don't care much about him.

Over time, GOP frustration mounted, the apparent benefits of cooperation decreased, and Gingrich's gospel of rebellion became more and more persuasive.

Like people, institutions are shaped by the major events of their lives.[19] In the case of the House, these events include a series of partisan battles, the most dramatic of which climaxed in the resignation of Speaker Jim Wright. Each incident seared the memories of Republicans and Democrats, coloring their vision of subsequent events. These fights also became part of the House's oral history, as veterans of both sides schooled their newcomers with partisan war stories. Gingrich benefitted on this account, because the emerging GOP history portrayed the Democrats as arrogant politicians who would yield to little except tough partisan pressure.

Academic analysts sometimes sniff that "mere anecdotes" can tell us little about Congress, but pivotal events change patterns of thought and action. The House GOP's recent history also suggests that we should regard preferences as fluid.

Remembering the Basics

The American political system's basic characteristics create dilemmas for the House Republicans. This system fosters both friction and fission. The friction results from the obstacles to rash action posed by the system's branches and layers. The fission consists of the system's openness, which allows for an energetic politics of ideas. The system curbs abuse of power while providing for its effective use; it limits change, yet permits constructive change.

Reflecting these two principles, Congress organizes along two conflicting lines. Congressional committees are poky vehicles that furnish economic interests and local constituencies with multiple veto points. Congressional parties, ideally, are vehicles for decisive change in the name of broad national interests. Party and committee organizations often compete, but in doing so they help Congress to balance party principles with parochial interests.

Lawmakers face "twin temptations." Some chafe at the friction of the constitutional system. They dream of grand ideological battles on the model of the New Deal, and are tempted by the system's potential for energy, or fission. In this, they echo the "party government" school of political science.[20] Others, echoing the "pluralist" school of political science, welcome the system's built-in friction. The House Republicans have been racked by conflict between the two sides, with the former lately gaining the upper hand.

Another point of contention emerges from the separation of powers. In a parliamentary system, the majority forms "the government" and the minority becomes "the loyal opposition." In the American system, "the government" includes all the members of all three branches, so the minority party in the House never has a perfectly neat choice between "government" and "opposition." It inevitably plays the role of both the minor partner in a coalition government and the opposition party. The closest it can come to the latter role is when the other party rules the White House and both chambers of Congress, or in other words, the circumstances that followed the 1992 election. Yet even then, the minority party's fate is bound to the rest of the government: a storm of anti-incumbency takes Republican victims as well as Democratic ones. Like it or not, the House GOP cannot "quit worrying about governing," as one top aide urged.

All House Republicans hear conflicting calls to duty. A sense of national responsibility may summon them to cooperate with the majority party to enact legislation for the common good. A sense of obligation to constituents and supporters may tug them toward serving parochial aims. Loyalty to a president of the same party may pull them in one direction, while loyalty to fellow Republicans in the House may pull in yet another. Because of such conflicts, the House Republicans often inflict more damage on themselves and their friends than on the Democrats. Bill Frenzel said: "House Republicans have so little and they always manage to lose it."

Getting the Story Straight

Even on its most straightforward level, this book's descriptive matter will correct misunderstandings and close gaps in the knowledge about the House GOP. Such tasks are prosaic but important, because the shortage of scholarly research has left many writers on Congress with a faulty picture of this topic. Two small examples illustrate the point. A number of works refer to the House GOP's campaign organization as the "Republican Congressional Campaign Committee" when its proper name is the National Republican Congressional Committee. Other works confuse the House Republican Research Committee (an official arm of the leadership) with the House Republican Study Committee (a legislative service organization for conservative members).

While such errors seem trifling, they suggest a clouded vision that has more serious consequences. Some observers describe the House Republicans as a unified bloc whose only disagreements turn on trivial matters. One essayist has written that the House GOP, with its "centralized, disciplined, organization, is far more like a European party than the Democratic Party is."[21] This is nonsense: the House Republicans' organization is anything but centralized and disciplined, and their frequent disarray reflects deep internal divisions.

The Puzzle of Minority Status

During their long time in the political wilderness, Republicans have seldom posed a serious threat to the Democratic majority. In 1956, the GOP came within seventeen seats of control, but lost forty-eight seats in the next election. Three times since (in 1968, 1972, and 1980), they have touched the "glass ceiling" of 192 seats (see Figure 1-2).

Why have they fallen so short for so long? House Republicans cannot agree on the sources of their difficulty. They are befuddled by the puzzle of minority status, because in many ways the 1980s appeared to be a Republican decade. The "Reagan Revolution" had politicians and political scientists talking about a party realignment similar to FDR's New Deal coalition. Voter identification with the GOP increased, as did the Republican presidential vote. Republicans captured and held the Senate for the first time in twenty-six years; and for most of the decade, their national party organizations seemed to have superior financial resources. But at the end of President George

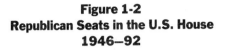

Figure 1-2
Republican Seats in the U.S. House
1946–92

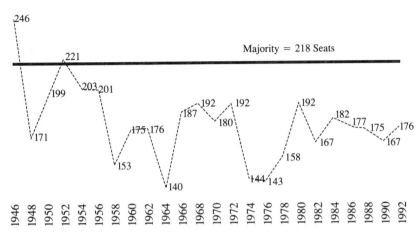

When the House temporarily expanded its membership to 437 after the admission of Alaska and Hawaii to statehood, a majority consisted of 219 members.

Bush's term, House Republicans were left with a net *loss* of sixteen seats since the election of 1980. What happened?

The House Republicans we interviewed offered many explanations. While they mentioned most of the elements that political scientists cite, they also identified reasons that the literature has tended to overlook. For convenience, we group these explanations under the headings "Damn Democrats" and "Damn Republicans."

Damn Democrats

Many contend that House Democrats have guarded their majority with various barriers and ruses. The 1992 Republican platform underscored this argument with purple prose:

> The Democrats have controlled the House of Representatives for 38 years—five years longer than Castro has held Cuba. They have held the Senate for 32 of those 38. Their entrenched power has produced a Congress arrogant, out of touch, hopelessly entangled in a web of PACs, perks, privileges, partisanship, paralysis and pork. . . . They have stacked campaign laws to benefit themselves. . . . After more than a half-

century of distortion by power-hungry Democrats, the political system is increasingly rigged. Throughout the 1980s, voters were cheated out of dozens of seats in the House of Representatives and in State legislatures because districts were oddly shaped to guarantee election of Democrats. It was swindle by law.[22]

House Republicans fume about the "Coelho-ization" of political action committees. In the early 1980s, they contend, Democratic Congressional Campaign Committee Chairman Tony Coelho (D-California) muscled the "wimpy" PAC community into putting its money at the disposal of Democratic incumbents. House Democratic "godfathers" chairing key committees or subcommittees have steered PAC money to needy rank-and-file Democrats and shut it off from GOP challengers.

Republicans also argue that the House Democrats are adept at pleasing local constituents with pork-barrel projects, and rewarding national voting blocs with social programs. Not only do the Democrats have the power of the purse, but their "big-government" enables them to argue that these expenditures are consistent with their vision of the public good. To some extent, the GOP overstates its case. Republicans, as well as Democrats, have benefitted from incumbency perquisites, well-targeted federal projects, and artful redistricting schemes. Yet as we shall see, the Republicans' argument does have some merit.

Damn Republicans

Congress scholars have often heard the House Republicans' complaints against the Democrats. What is less familiar is the depth of GOP self-criticism.

Some favor a "political" rather than "structural" explanation for their minority status. Like political scientist Gary Jacobson, they say that Republicans remain in the minority because they nominate weak candidates on the wrong side of the issues.[23] Jacobson insists that the limited experience and funding of GOP challengers relative to their Democratic counterparts makes for generally "poor quality" candidates. Some House Republicans blame this problem on their party's failings at the state and local level. They note sadly that state GOP organizations have "atrophied" in recent decades, and that the Republican state legislators provide a limited pool for recruiting congressional challengers. The Democrats, as the "party of government," are better able to recruit challengers. "You can't beat somebody with nobody," all agree. Even those candidates Republicans do recruit are handicapped because of GOP "litmus tests" among state and local activists.

A number of House Republicans cited the GOP's general weakness on domestic issues. Some said that their party lacks a "governing conservatism" that promotes positive ("magnet") alternatives to attract both voters and candidates. Other House Republicans, especially within the party's conservative ranks, argued that the GOP basic philosophy is fine, but that Republicans have failed to articulate it in terms that move the voters.

The similarity between the arguments of politicians and political analysts is no coincidence. Most Washington aides and consultants have had political science courses as part of their undergraduate or graduate training, and some even have doctorates. Moreover, many members and staff like to follow readable accounts of research that affects them. During the time of our interviews, many Washington figures—including some of our interview subjects—were reading Alan Ehrenhalt's *The United States of Ambition*.[24] We heard echoes of Ehrenhalt's conclusion that the professionalization of American politics has altered Congress. We even encountered the suggestion that low Capitol Hill salaries, compared with potential private-sector jobs, hurt Republican recruiting and staff hiring efforts more than Democratic ones.

Some House Republicans saw many GOP incumbents as too "fat, dumb, and happy" to work for majority status. Others said the House GOP is given to hurtful mood swings, from despair to manic optimism and back again. We repeatedly heard that House Republicans lack serious governing experience, "all talk and no action." House Democrats frequently echo this latter criticism, for they regard the minority as irredeemably irresponsible.

Rank-and-file Republicans denounced ranking minority members of standing committees for ignoring the rest of the House GOP. They also faulted the party leadership's structure and personnel as "flawed." Different factions usually chose different leaders to rebuke. Michel's defenders blamed Gingrich's "bombthrowing," and Gingrich's friends pointed to Michel's alleged complacency.

The National Republican Congressional Committee (NRCC) came in for a stunning amount of censure. The most common complaints involved its centralized bureaucracy and its dependence on high-paid staffers and consultants. House GOP critics of NRCC also damned the organization as being top-heavy with "contributors' sons and daughters." Other charges included inept targeting of races and poor recruitment of candidates.

Three things may be said in NRCC's defense. First, much of the GOP's difficulty lies beyond the reach of Washington operatives, even though some would-be strategists remain invincibly ignorant about their own limitations. Second, House Republicans seemed to know little about this organization operating across the street from their offices. When questioned, they sometimes blamed this ignorance on the NRCC itself. Third, at the time we were finishing this book, the organization had slimmed down to the point of anorexia.

Even GOP presidential successes brought sighs from House Republicans. The Reagan-Bush years, some think, resulted in a "talent drain" of potential recruits and aspiring leaders. In the waning days of the Bush administration, Gingrich called the executive branch "a vacuum cleaner for potential GOP candidates." Other members noted with regret that leaders Dick Cheney, Jack Kemp, Lynn Martin, and Edward Madigan all ended up in the Cabinet. In particular, Gingrich saw Cheney's move as a terrible blow to House Republican fortunes. Of course, Cheney's departure also opened up the whip's job for Gingrich.

Prescription Meets Diagnosis:
Just What the Spin Doctor Ordered

In the 1980s and early 1990s, observers offered various remedies for the House GOP, some of which seemed more workable than others.

During the time of GOP White House rule, political scientist Thomas Mann observed that because the party of the White House tended to lose congressional seats over time, the Republicans could not win a majority in the House of Representatives until their party lost the presidency.[25] In 1992, although they could do little to affect the outcome either way, some House Republicans quietly hoped for Bush's defeat. During an interview in 1992, a conservative House Republican leader voiced optimism about the upcoming election. He seemed confident that the freshman class would teem with activist conservatives. He hedged on whether he wanted Bush to lose: "We win either way."

A number of House Republicans despised the "win by losing" strategy, seeing the Reagan and Bush presidencies as the only barrier between them and irrelevancy. Barber Conable said: "If you're a 'permanent minority,' or just a minority, and you don't have the White House, you don't have anything. The White House needed the Republican members of Ways and Means, but I needed the White House even more." A top GOP committee staffer insisted Michel was right to see himself as the "point man" for Republican presidents since they are "the best thing we've got." The same aide scorned Newt Gingrich and others who think they can "make policy as a minority of the lower house."

The mirror image of the "lose the White House" strategy is the "Truman strategy" that Washington conservatives urged upon George Bush. A year before the 1948 election, White House aide James Rowe wrote a memo urging Truman to confront the Republican majority in Congress by championing a clear liberal agenda. Whether at Rowe's advice or by his own instinct, Truman pursued this line of attack against the "do-nothing" Congress and thus helped end the House Republicans' reign. Forty-four years later, confrontational Republicans touted the Rowe memo in hopes that Bush would take on the Democratic Congress. He largely ignored their counsel. Even his long string of sustained vetoes was less impressive than it seemed because he seldom vetoed legislation unless he knew in advance that he already had enough votes to block an override. And when he did veto bills, he passed up the opportunity to put forth an alternative agenda, rather than just block Democratic initiatives.[26] Accordingly, his eleventh-hour invocation of Harry Truman sounded hollow.

The "Truman strategy" was a special case of debate over party strategy. For years, one side has hoped to turn House elections into referenda on broad national concerns, and to peel away Democratic voters by stressing "wedge" issues. The other side, thinking that "all politics is local," has argued that House Republicans must emphasize community concerns to win seats one by one, district by district. Some want to concentrate on changing the public's preferences over the long term, even at the expense of current policy deadlock, while others want to affect policy now, even at the expense of long-term partisan gains.

The Structure of this Book

Some books about Congress focus on campaigns and elections, while others focus on the inner workings of Capitol Hill. This book considers both. In Chapters 2 and 3, we look at the House GOP's composition and leadership structure, drawing from the literature on congressional parties. In Chapter 4, we turn to the relationship between the majority and minority parties in the House: here we rely on institutional histories and studies of congressional procedure. In Chapter 5, we start to analyze the causes of the House GOP's minority status. This chapter taps a wide array of sources to explain how the GOP's electoral problems are rooted in interests, institutions, ideas and individuals. In Chapter 6, we continue our explanation of minority status, concentrating on survey research and voting data. In Chapter 7, we explore how strategies fit with diagnoses. There may be no single solution to the puzzle. A more complete knowledge of context is a key to understanding the House Republicans' central problem.

We hope to fill a large gap in the literature by focusing on a topic that scholars have ignored for too long. Again, Charles O. Jones wrote *the* book on this subject a generation ago. Since then, the House Republicans' minority status has changed from a normal phase of the political cycle to an unprecedented forty-year phenomenon. In this book, we seek to update the record and correct any myths about the House Republicans and their unique situation. Above all, we want to encourage further discussion about a topic that can shed light on congressional behavior and general American politics.

Notes

1. Republicans formally yielded control of the House on January 3, 1955. As of 1991, slightly more than 55 percent of Americans had been born since that date. Calculated from: U.S. Department of Commerce, Bureau of the Census, *Statistical Abstract of the United States 1992* (Washington, D.C.: Government Printing Office, 1992), 15.

2. Charles O. Jones, *The Minority Party in Congress* (Boston: Little, Brown, 1970). Subsequent books have dealt with the House GOP, though not as their focus. See A. James Reichley, *Conservatives in an Era of Change* (Washington, D.C.: Brookings, 1981); Nicol Rae, *The Decline and Fall of the Liberal Republicans From 1952 to the Present* (New York: Oxford University Press, 1989). For a study of a single GOP faction, see Edwin J. Feulner, Jr., *Conservatives Stalk the House: The Republican Study Committee 1970–1982* (Ottawa, Ill.: Green Hill, 1983). For a contemporary sketch, see John B. Bader and Charles O. Jones, "The Republican Parties in Congress: Bicameral Differences," in *Congress Reconsidered*, 5th ed., ed. Lawrence C. Dodd and Bruce I. Oppenheimer (Washington, D.C.: CQ Press, 1993), 291–313.

3. Walter B. Roettger and Hugh Winebrenner, "Politics and Political Scientists," *Public Opinion*, September/October 1986, 41–44.

4. R. Douglas Arnold, "Overtilled and Undertilled Fields in American Politics," *Political Science Quarterly* 97 (Spring 1982): 91–103.

5. Richard F. Fenno, Jr., *Congressmen in Committees* (Boston: Little, Brown, 1973).

6. Charles O. Jones, "Joseph G. Cannon and Howard W. Smith: An Essay on the Limits of Leadership in the House of Representatives," in *Congressional Behavior*, ed. Nelson W. Polsby (New York: Random House, 1971), 203–24.

7. Barbara Sinclair, "The Evolution of Party Leadership in the Modern House," in *The Atomistic Congress: An Interpretation of Congressional Change*, ed. Allen D. Hertzke and Ronald M. Peters, Jr. (Armonk, N.Y.: M. E. Sharpe, 1992), 259–92.

8. Quoted in Jeffrey H. Birnbaum, "House Republicans, Frustrated in Minority Role, Often Ask Themselves Whether It's Time to Leave," *Wall Street Journal*, June 5, 1987, 52.

9. For another discussion of individual and party goals, see: R. Douglas Arnold, *The Logic of Congressional Action* (New Haven: Yale University Press, 1990), 266.

10. Quoted in Janet Hook, "House GOP: Plight of a Permanent Minority," *Congressional Quarterly Weekly Report*, June 21, 1986, 1393.

11. Quoted in Birnbaum, "House Republicans, Frustrated," 52.

12. James MacGregor Burns, *Leadership* (New York: Harper and Row/ Harper Colophon, 1979), 344–68.

13. James Q. Wilson, "The Politics of Regulation," in *The Politics of Regulation*, ed. James Q. Wilson (New York: Basic, 1980), 363.

14. *Congressional Record*, daily ed., September 12, 1989, E3001.

15. James Ceaser and Andrew Busch, *Upside Down and Inside Out: The 1992 Elections and American Politics* (Lanham, Md.: Rowman and Littlefield/ Littlefield Adams Quality Paperbacks, 1993), 2.

16. James W. Ceaser, "The City and The Country in the American Tradition," *Journal of Political Science* 15 (Spring 1987): 21–35.

17. "The most important strategy in politics is concerned with the scope of conflict." E. E. Schattschneider, *The Semi-Sovereign People: A Realist's View of Democracy in America* (Hinsdale, Ill.: Dryden, 1960), 3.

18. Joseph Cooper and David W. Brady, "Institutional Context and Leadership Style: The House from Cannon to Rayburn," *American Political Science Review* 75 (June 1981): 411–25.

19. Richard E. Neustadt and Ernest R. May, *Thinking in Time: The Uses of History for Decision Makers* (New York: Free Press, 1986), 212.

20. The classic statement of the "party government" school is: Committee on Political Parties, American Political Science Association, *Toward a More Responsible Two-Party System* (New York: Rinehart, 1950).

21. Michael Lind, "A Radical Plan to Change American Politics," *Atlantic Monthly*, August 1992, 78.

22. Republican National Convention, *The Vision Shared: Uniting Our Family, Our Country, Our World* (Houston: Republican National Convention, 1992), 67–71.

23. Gary C. Jacobson, *The Electoral Origins of Divided Government* (Boulder, Colo.: Westview, 1990).

24. Alan Ehrenhalt, *The United States of Ambition: Politicians, Power and the Pursuit of Office* (New York: Random House/Times Books, 1991).

25. Thomas E. Mann, "Is the House of Representatives Unresponsive to Political Change?" in *Elections American Style*, ed. A. James Reichley (Washington, D.C.: Brookings, 1987), 277.

26. Charles Kolb, *White House Daze: The Unmaking of Domestic Policy in the Bush Years* (New York: Free Press, 1994), 11; Terry Eastland, *Energy in the Executive: The Case for a Strong Presidency* (New York: Free Press, 1992), 117.

Chapter 2

Family Feuds

At first glance, House Republicans seem a bland lot. At the start of the 103d Congress, only 2.3 percent of House Republicans were black or Latino, compared with 20.9 percent of the Democrats.[1] Republicans also have a narrower electoral base, winning relatively few poor or urban districts. This plain-vanilla face might suggest that the House Republicans think alike, act like, and get along with one another.[2]

Appearances deceive. As James Madison wrote, the causes of faction are "sown in the nature of man" and include leadership rivalries, policy disputes, and divergent economic interests, to name a few.[3] Such differences churn the House Republicans, leading to lively quarrels that bear only a faint resemblance to the internal disputes on the other side of the aisle. Not only do the two parties have distinct social bases, they have different things to argue about: while the majority members debate how to govern the country, the minority members must debate how to cope with their lowly place in the House.

This chapter identifies the party's major divisions and explains how they have shaped GOP behavior. We look both at organizations such as the Conservative Opportunity Society, as well as broad groupings based on attitude and background. A customary way of analyzing legislative factions is to sort party members into a small set of mutually exclusive boxes; however, this approach would yield a flat and distorted picture of the House Republicans. Instead, it is more useful to picture their differences as having layers, much like a set of transparencies on a demographic map. Each layer has its own dividing line, which is jagged, shifting, and only roughly similar to the dividing lines of the other layers.

The following pairings suggest the various levels on which House Republicans part company:

West and South	vs.	Northeast and Midwest
Younger	vs.	Older
Party Activists	vs.	"District Guys" and "Committee Guys"
"Bombthrowers"	vs.	'Responsible Partners in Governing"
Conservatives	vs.	Moderates
Congressional GOP Loyalists	vs.	Presidential GOP Loyalists
Supporters of "National Strategy"	vs.	Supporters of "Local Strategy"

The groups on the left-hand side (though not the political left!) tend to favor Gingrich and those on the other side tend to oppose him. But this "Great Divide" is a great oversimplification: many members stand on one side at some levels while standing on the opposite side at other levels. During the 1980s, for instance, Mickey Edwards (R-Oklahoma) headed the American Conservative Union, but he also denounced Gingrich's confrontational tactics. Nancy Johnson (R-Connecticut) has a moderate voting record, but she is also a party activist who has sometimes stood in Gingrich's corner.

On each level, the divisions fluctuate when newcomers arrive, veterans leave, or attitudes shift. Preferences are flexible: though members seldom move from one state to another, they do change their minds about policy and political strategy.

While the House GOP's splits might seem obscure to outsiders, the members take them seriously. A religious analogy drives home the point. A Moslem may see little difference between Protestants and Catholics, just as a Christian may equate Sunnis with Shiites. But these distinctions mean life or death on the streets of Belfast and Baghdad.

Republican versus Republican

Northeast and Midwest vs. South and West

Since the founding of the Republican Party, most of its House members had always come from the Northeast and Midwest.[4] From the 1960s through the 1980s, these regions suffered a net loss of seats to the West and South, and Republicans gained a foothold in the latter region, which had once sent near-solid Democratic delegations to the House. Such trends caused a regional power shift among House Republicans. Over time, the West and South claimed an increasing share of Republican members, and with the start of the 103d Congress in 1993, these regions accounted for a substantial majority of the House GOP (Figure 2-1).

In previous decades, the Northeast and Midwest had supplied the

Figure 2-1
Regional Representation Among House Republicans
91st through 103d Congresses

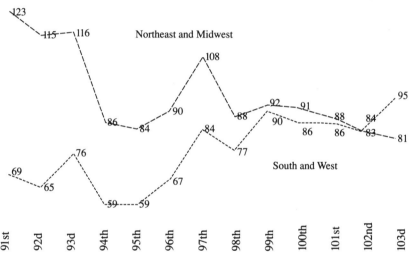

Data refer to the total number of Republican House members from the Northeast and Midwest, and from the South and West. In this book, we follow the census definition of regions:

Northeast: Connecticut, Maine, Massachusetts, New Hampshire, New Jersey, New York, Pennsylvania, Rhode Island, Vermont.

Midwest: Illinois, Indiana, Iowa, Kansas, Michigan, Minnesota, Missouri, Nebraska, North Dakota, Ohio, South Dakota, Wisconsin.

South: Alabama, Arkansas, Delaware, Florida, Georgia, Kentucky, Louisana, Maryland, Mississippi, North Carolina, Oklahoma, South Carolina, Tennessee, Texas, Virginia, West Virginia.

West: Alaska, Arizona, California, Colorado, Hawaii, Idaho, Montana, New Mexico, Nevada, Oregon, Utah, Washington, Wyoming.

Source: Adapted from U.S. Department of Commerce, Bureau of the Census, *Statistical Abstract of the United States,* various years.

House GOP Conference with a significant number of liberal members, who wielded a modicum of influence over Republican policy. As the 1990s began, however, the more-conservative South and West were defining House Republicanism.

Indeed, northeastern Republicans were starting to fill an odd niche once occupied by southern Democrats. Whereas Southerners used to break frequently from their fellow Democrats, the 1980s saw the proportion of southern Democrats with low unity scores shrink to vanishing levels.[5] As Table 2-1 shows, more than half of the northeast-erners had 1991 party unity scores under 70, compared with less than a tenth of the Republicans from elsewhere. New York State was home to six of the ten lowest-scoring House Republicans. By 1993, however, New York had lost the relative strength it had once enjoyed. California had long surpassed it in population, and the House GOP Conference now had just as many Floridians (thirteen) as New Yorkers.

Younger vs. Older

During the 1960s and 1970s, Congress was populated mainly by the World War II generation: members born before 1930. In 1979, they still made up more than half of the GOP Conference. The relentless hand of demography then started to move them from the scene. By 1993, only one-sixth of the House Republicans belonged to the GI genera-tion, while more than a third were "baby boomers," born after 1945.

The younger members differ from the GI generation in their appetite for publicity, their orientation to national-issue constituencies, and their willingness to work at the expense of comity and compromise.[6] During the 1960s, Gerald Ford and other Republicans of the World War

Table 2-1
1991 Party Unity Scores Among House Republicans, by Region

	Northeast (N = 37)		Midwest (N = 45)		South (N = 47)		West (N = 37)	
90–100	8%	(3)	18%	(8)	40%	(19)	59%	(22)
80–89	19%	(7)	49%	(22)	36%	(17)	24%	(9)
70–79	22%	(8)	20%	(9)	19%	(9)	11%	(4)
60–69	24%	(9)	11%	(5)	0		3%	(1)
Under 60	27%	(10)	2%	(1)	4%	(2)	3%	(1)

Source: Authors' calculation from *Congressional Quarterly Weekly Report*, December 28, 1991, 3790–91.

II generation did work hard to develop party policy. Still youthful enough to be called "Young Turks," they displayed more energy than their predecessors. Their proposals, however, tended to be cut-rate versions of Democratic initiatives. More important, their political style emphasized conciliation and moderation: Ford was no more likely to attack Democratic Speakers John McCormack or Carl Albert than they were to attack him.

During the 1980s, Republican members of all ages felt the constraints of minority status, but different generations reacted in different ways. The older Republicans—the "Young Turks" of two decades before— still tended to seek accommodation. The younger Republicans articulated their views in manifestoes, press releases, and television appearances. And when they thought Democratic leaders behaved unfairly or unethically, they attacked: witness the downfall of Speaker Jim Wright.

Time has been obliterating the House GOP's "institutional memory" of the days of comity and nonideological compromise. For more and more House Republicans, partisan rancor and policy ferment have flavored their experience of the chamber. Of the 176 Republicans who took the oath of office in January 1993:

- Only *fourteen* had served under Gerald Ford's House GOP leadership;

- Only *sixteen* had served under any House speaker before Tip O'Neill;

- Only *thirty-two* had served under any president before Reagan.[7]

In the early 1980s, some observers speculated that the "generation gap" would prove fleeting, and that as the younger members gained seniority and paunch, they would return to the ways of their elders. Generational differences have largely defied these forecasts: despite more than a decade of seniority, Gingrich and his original cohort of allies are still far more media-oriented and confrontational than Michel. At the same time, the years have slightly smoothed their edges, and some of the newer members are outdoing them. Shortly before announcing his retirement, Michel called the current GOP Conference "the most conservative and antagonistic to the other side" that he had ever seen. Of the forty-seven freshmen, he said, "seven are thoughtful moderates, and the other forty are pretty darn hard-liners, some of them real hard line."[8]

Richard Pombo (R-California), born in 1961, exemplifies the class of 1992. "A lot of leaders are satisfied with the way things work," he said. "The longer you're here, the less of a problem you see with the way it's being run."[9] During markup of the 1993 tax bill, he led fourteen other freshmen in a press conference outside the Ways and Means Committee door. Protesting the committee's decision to meet in closed-door session, Pombo and his colleagues put up a sign that read: "Do Not Disturb! Democrats Raising Taxes!" In June 1993, the United States Business and Industrial Council recognized his antitax position by awarding him a pair of boxing gloves, which he prominently displayed on the wall behind his desk.

Party Activists vs. "District Guys" and "Committee Guys"

Every House Republican represents a local constituency, serves on one or more committees, and belongs to the party conference. According to Gingrich, minority members find it quite a challenge to concentrate on their partisan role:

> First of all, it takes a fairly strong ego to think you have a direct relationship to an issue as large as becoming a majority. Second, none of the social and institutional reward systems are related to the majoritarian status. And third you're faced with the active hostility of most of the press, most of the lobbyists, all of the Democrats, and about a third of the Republicans.

Nevertheless, a number of Republicans do maintain an interest in building a majority. How many such members are there? Gingrich said in 1992 that "the number of people in elected office who think consistently about becoming a majority is somewhere between one and five. There are another fifty or sixty who think about it occasionally." He added that sentiment had shifted since the late 1970s, "when a majority of the caucus preferred passively accepting Democratic dominance." Nowadays, "there are more people who are glad we're thinking about [majority status] and fewer people who are angry that we're thinking about it."

The activists' ranks grew further with the 1992 election, which brought in a large number of new members who were not yet caught up in the House's incentive system. It remains difficult, however, to pin down a precise percentage. According to a former member of the GOP leadership:

It fluctuates over time, and it's also to some extent related to how safe the House member's district is. . . . There's not a perfect correlation there, but it's a lot easier for a guy to be willing to go to war if he's not that worried about getting re-elected. I would put Newt right at the top of the list of those guys who are primarily interested in the majority and a national strategy. That's one of his strengths. That's what he always brings to the fray. But it's a lot tougher for a member to get caught up in all of that, if in fact he's got a tough district or reelection campaign back home.

No member can think about majority status every minute. Even Gingrich has had to spend some of his time tending to his constituency (especially since his 1990 near-defeat), and his opponents have attacked him for talking about deficit spending while seeking benefits for Cobb County, Georgia.[10] In 1990, Republican Conference Chairman Jerry Lewis (R-California) pondered the dilemma of being both an economy-minded party leader and an Appropriations Committee member from economically troubled California: "I find myself almost in conflict with myself. I believe in the free market economy. . . . On the other hand, I live in a district that was built on the largesse of the federal government. Too quick a shrinkage could cause pain on top of what is already there, so I am trying to work with local communities in dealing with the transition. And thus a moderate Republican is born."[11]

Many other Republicans simply disregard this dilemma by putting other considerations ahead of party. Bud Shuster (R-Pennsylvania) once chaired the House GOP Policy Committee, but after he lost a 1980 bid for the chair of the Republican Conference, he began to focus heavily on the needs of his district. From his seat on the constituency-oriented Public Works Committee, he has worked to bring home construction projects—including the Bud Shuster By-Way. "There's no such thing as a Republican or Democratic bridge," he said in 1993, "or a Republican or Democratic airport."[12]

Over time, some Republicans start to identify primarily with their committees, or as a longtime Republican committee aide said in 1987: "You begin to think of yourself as an Energy and Commerce or a Merchant Marine person." Carlos Moorhead (R-California), who became ranking Republican on Energy and Commerce in 1993, shrugged off suggestions that he would defer to chairman John Dingell: "It isn't a sin to work with the people who have a majority vote if we can come up with a product that's satisfactory to our people."[13] Bill Goodling (R-Pennsylvania), ranking Republican on Education and Labor, breaks with the Democratic majority on labor issues, but pursues "our bipartisan bit" on education policy, irritating Republicans who want to make a national issue of education reform.[14]

According to party activist Bob Walker (R-Pennsylvania), such proclivities cause problems for House Republicans:

> We've had an attitude among many of our more senior members that because they didn't see any way out of minority status, that they found it easier to cooperate with Democrats to get a percentage of the action in the House rather than presenting alternatives, and so . . . much of what came to the floor ended up being bipartisan in nature as it came out of the committee. The only people fighting the committees tended to be people from off the committees, and so . . . we had no real case to take to the country.

The difference in perspective extends to the staff level. Said a former leadership aide: "There is a big gap between the leadership staff and the committee staff. They're looking in different directions. It's as if you and I were standing in a room talking to each other, but facing two different walls." According to Gingrich, communication and coordination become a problem: "It's almost a contest between farmers and nomads . . . there's the different lifestyles, different patterns, different ways. If you are a staffer whose entire life is a subcommittee, and you spent years mastering every important detail, in my mind you're a resource person. In your mind, I'm an interloper."

By 1993, committee-oriented members had declining influence within GOP ranks. In the organizing sessions for the 103d Congress—with freshmen casting a quarter of the vote—the House Republicans reined in committee members in several ways:

- By a vote of 82-44, they forbade anyone in the Conference from holding the post of ranking committee member for more than six years in a row.

- They also passed a rule requiring ranking members to work with the leadership in drafting written plans for dealing with key issues.

- Within the Committee on Committees, activists sought to depose several ranking members. The effort fell short but served a symbolic purpose. Said Gerald Solomon (New York): "Really, this was a message to the ranking members that they serve the Republican Conference."[15]

"Bombthrowers" vs. "Responsible Partners in Governing"

One party leader put the "great divide" among House Republicans in these terms: "The cleavage is between those favoring confrontation, the risk-takers, and the responsible partners in governing." He added: "The public would be startled to discover how nonpolitical most members of Congress are . . . for them there is a disconnect between politics and government." He proudly proclaimed, "I'm a politician." The confrontationists, or "bombthrowers," insist their approach serves a constructive purpose: through "confrontation, confrontation, confrontation" and by "polarizing issues" they "sharpen the differences between the two parties." Theirs is an ideological politics of combat.

The bombthrowers frequently attack the majority's record, and Democrats accuse them of being anti-Congress. In response to such criticism, Gingrich said: "No, I'm anti-corruption, and I'm anti-Democratic control. I'm pro-Congress." He rebuffed his critics' charge that he wants to destroy the institution:

> No, only if they define the institution as corrupt and Democratic. I mean, if by the institution they mean the current model of Democratic control of the House, the current one-sided control of the Rules Committee, the current rigging of the rules, the current liberal domination of scheduling and the current one-sided stamping on behalf of the Democrats, then yes, I'm interested in breaking up the Democratic monopoly of power.

Although some of Gingrich's allies distance themselves from his ethics battles, many share his antiestablishment perspective and speak the language of outsiderism. One said: "What we need today is Ronald Reagan in 1980. The result could be a huge partisan victory based on an anti-government, outsider campaign." Another called the Democratic Congress "the single most reactionary institution in the country today."

The bombthrower wing took organizational shape in 1983, when Gingrich and other junior Republicans formed the Conservative Opportunity Society (COS), a group devoted to sharpening partisan distinctions on the House floor. During the next couple of years, COS gained attention for its C-SPAN-broadcast "special order" speeches damning Democratic leaders. Though some observers initially dismissed COS, it left an impact on the GOP. By 1989, half of the eight elected Republican leaders were COS veterans.

Over time, some of the original COS figures became less active in the group as they went on to GOP leadership posts. Others were elected to the Senate (Connie Mack of Florida and Dan Coats of Indiana) or other offices (Dan Lungren of California became the state's attorney general). By the 102d Congress, COS's active membership consisted mostly of lawmakers who had entered Congress since the group's founding. Although the COS membership list is confidential, interviews and observation suggest that the active members included the following: Chairman Jim Bunning (R-Kentucky, elected to Congress 1988), Newt Gingrich (R-Georgia, 1978), Cass Ballenger (R-North Carolina, 1986), Mel Hancock (R-Missouri, 1988), Toby Roth (R-Wisconsin, 1978), Andy Ireland (R-Florida, 1976), Jon Kyl (R-Arizona, 1986), Craig Thomas (R-Wyoming, 1989), Robert Walker (R-Pennsylvania, 1976), Christopher Cox (R-California, 1988), Ileana Ros-Lehtinen (R-Florida, 1989) and Dana Rohrabacher (R-California, 1988).

In recent years, COS has concentrated less on C-SPAN speeches. Instead, working with deputy whip Walker, it has focused on floor debate and parliamentary tactics. According to one former aide, COS members believe they made a significant difference in the repeal both of catastrophic health insurance and of Section 89 of the 1986 tax overhaul (dealing with employee benefits). In the 103d Congress, under the chairmanship of John Boehner (R-Ohio), COS fought the Clinton budget proposals by supporting a bold spending-cut plan offered by John Kasich (R-Ohio).

COS has not been the only organized group within the GOP. The 92 Group, named for the year of the hoped-for GOP majority, aimed to make Republicans responsible partners in governing. The 92 Group was organized in 1985 by Olympia Snowe (R-Maine), Tom Tauke (R-Iowa), and about three dozen other Republicans, with the idea of providing a counterweight to COS. As Tauke explained: "There is a difference of opinion on strategy. One school says to let Democrats sink in their own soup. Others say the best way is to clarify our own position . . . I think that it is important to clarify our own view."[16] An aide to a 92 Group member was more blunt: "We needed a more thoughtful approach than just scream and yell on the floor."

The 92 Group tried to redefine the GOP image by drafting proposals that might pass the House. Its bent was best captured by a 1985 comment from Carl Pursell (R-Michigan). The group had drafted a budget that would curb spending while avoiding wholesale termination of social programs. "Good news," Pursell told a 92 Group meeting, "[Budget Chairman William] Gray just told me that their budget would be 80 to 90 percent of our budget. He asked if we could live with that, and I told him we'd take a look at it.''[17]

The Northeast and Midwest accounted for about three-fourths of the members of the 92 Group, while the South and West contributed the bulk of the COS members. Long before the 1992 election, the 92 Group had petered out, a victim of regional shifts, the bombthrowers' growing influence, and the increasingly rancorous politics of the federal budget, which worked against bipartisan compromise.

The bombthrower/responsible partner division encompasses more than the differences between COS and the 92 Group. Some of the voices for the latter viewpoint have come from other quarters. In 1984, conservative Oklahoman Mickey Edwards issued an attack on COS: "But those of us who actually want to achieve a government predicated on these conservative viewpoints, those of us who want results and not just rhetoric, must work with the Democrats, with the Senate and with the White House to achieve as much as we can, as fast as we can, moving incrementally toward success, rather than attempting to burn down the Capitol and point the finger at Democrats, saying, 'They started it.' ''[18]

The debate between bombthrowers and responsible partners has hinged on whether House Republicans have any real influence. One ranking member with a reputation for clout said that House Republicans suffer from a "self-fulfilling prophecy" of impotence, although he acknowledged a serious limit on his ability to influence Democratic committee colleagues, and soon after our interview he left the House.

Despite their differences over confrontational tactics, some bombthrowers and "responsible partners" share an interest in policy innovation. As COS chairman Boehner put it: "Unless you offer an alternative, you are not meeting your responsibility."[19] In the late 1980s and early 1990s, the House Wednesday Group supplied a forum for communication between both sides. Originally a bastion of northeastern liberals, the Wednesday Group later expanded to include members such as Vin Weber (R-Minnesota), a founder of COS. Shortly after his election as whip, Gingrich observed: "There is almost a new synthesis evolving with the classic moderate wing of the party, where, as a former Rockefeller state chairman, I've spent most of my life, and the conservative/activist wing."[20] One example of this synthesis is the successful effort of "responsible partner" Thomas Petri (R-Wisconsin) to expand the Earned Income Tax Credit, a policy that dovetails with the increasingly popular conservative concept of "empowerment."

It would be an overstatement to claim that these efforts at synthesis have erased the Republicans' ideological lines. Policy disagreements continue to plague them.

Conservatives vs. Moderates

Through the 1960s, the House GOP included a fair number of liberals. Though this wing never dominated the Conference, it did supply the party with articulate voices such as John Anderson (R-Illinois) and John Lindsay (R-New York), who later became a target of conservative anger as mayor of New York. The ideological balance shifted in the 1970s (Table 2-2). Strong conservatives gained a very clear majority, while strong liberals practically disappeared.

The growth of the Republican Study Committee (RSC) underscores the conservative shift. Formed in 1973 as a conservative Republican counterpart to the Democratic Study Group, RSC started with a few dozen members, but by the early 1990s, nearly three-quarters of House Republicans were members.[21] RSC serves mainly to provide its members with legislative updates, background papers, and customized research; some members belong less to advance ideological aims than to make use of RSC services. The RSC staff shuns reporters and scholars, so it is difficult to appraise the group's role.

Table 2-2
Republican Ideological Divisions in the House of Representatives, 1969–91

| | Conservative Coalition Support Score | | | |
	1969	1979	1989	1991
84–100%	89 (47%)	104 (65%)	126 (76%)	130 (78%)
70–84%	42 (22%)	31 (19%)	33 (20%)	23 (14%)
55–59%	25 (13%)	9 (6%)	7 (4%)	11 (7%)
Under 55%	33 (17%)	15 (9%)	10 (6%)	2 (1%)
Total	189	159	176	166

The data come from *Congressional Quarterly's* Conservative Coalition support scores. They have been normalized to take account of absences. That is, normalized scores equal support scores divided by the sum of support and opposition scores. Because of this normalization, the data and categories differ slightly from those used in earlier studies. Total numbers of GOP members differ slightly from other tables because these figures are based on membership at the *end* of each year.

It is clear, however, that the Reagan era crushed most of the embers of old-style economic liberalism within the House GOP. In 1991, only a single House Republican (Benjamin Gilman of New York) scored over 50 percent on *National Journal*'s economic liberalism ratings.[22] But while one can spot few true liberals in Republican ranks, the party does split over social issues such as abortion.

For most of the 1980s, most House Republicans voted for restrictions on abortion. The GOP conference also had a small but vocal prochoice faction, so party leaders hesitated to take official party positions on the issue. According to Vin Weber: "There was never a House Republican agenda that came forward that included the right to life. It's been part of our [national party] platform. We basically leave it at that level within the party, and to the vast majority of right-to-life leaders, that's an appropriate position for our party to take."[23]

Individual members were less cautious. In 1992, Robert Dornan (R-California) presented a special order in which he held up a photograph of a fetus to the television camera and said: "[A]re you listening, Susan Molinari [R- New York]? If anybody in Susie Molinari's office is watching, call her to the television, Mr. Speaker, so she can see this. The same in Tommy Campbell's office, one of our California freshmen."[24] The next day, Molinari replied: "Mr. Speaker, I truly respect every one of my colleagues who is pro-life, their opinions, and their commitment. Congressman Dornan, I believe I deserve the same."[25]

Republican differences about abortion hinge on the framing of the issue. In March 1993, the House voted for a family-planning authorization bill that codified President Clinton's decision to lift the "gag rule" that had forbidden staff at federally funded clinics from discussing abortion with patients. Republicans, who split 51-121 against the measure, showed less unity than the Democrats, who voted 221-28 in favor.[26] A few months later, however, Republicans voted 157-16 for the Hyde amendment to prohibit Medicaid funding of abortion except in cases of rape, incest, or necessity to save the mother's life. While 154 Democrats voted against the amendment, 99 voted in favor, enough to put it over the top.[27]

The division goes beyond abortion to more general social attitudes. At a 1991 GOP retreat, one outside speaker blamed single-parent families for "crime, drugs, violence, disease, and Democrats." While a number of members applauded, Connie Morella (R-Maryland) was "shocked and appalled." Fred Grandy (R-Iowa) said to Morella's husband: "Did Connie violate some kind of Republican ethic by not staying home with the kids? I kind of worry when there's this Shiite cast to this meeting."[28]

Conservatives are themselves divided. Some want the party to emphasize opposition to abortion and gay rights. Others, while casting conservative votes on these issues, would rather stress economics. As mentioned earlier, some conservatives work with liberals on "new ideas" while others look with skepticism on any such effort. A leading figure of the latter group is Gerald Solomon (R-New York), who once explained, "I'm not what you'd call the New Right. I'm the Old Right."[29]

The issue of South Africa created a breach between the two groups. In 1984, Weber joined thirty-four other Republicans in sending a blunt anti-apartheid letter to the South African ambassador. Weber saw the letter as an effort to improve the GOP's image on race relations. "It's an unfortunate fact of life that conservative philosophy has often been twisted into a defense of discrimination and racism. We must rid ourselves of that legacy." Solomon, on the other hand, referred to the letter as "completely half-baked—counterproductive to what the [Reagan] administration is trying to accomplish."[30]

In 1992, Weber looked back on the debate: "I still think we had a legitimate argument about South Africa, which I've had with my conservative friends since December 1984. There have been times when we've been too tactical, and we've sacrificed some principle for a perceived tactical advantage. And that was probably a mistake."[31]

Congressional GOP Loyalists vs. Presidential GOP Loyalists

Any Republican president is doomed to an awkward relationship with a House GOP minority. To pass legislation, the White House has to work with the majority; but it occasionally needs the minority to sustain vetoes. House Republicans like access to executive branch officials, but they dislike being excluded from key negotiations and being asked to cast difficult votes for the president.

During the Reagan and Bush administrations, Republicans sometimes split badly on White House relations. In 1991, Republican Leader Michel voiced the view of the presidential loyalists: "George Bush is still our president for another two years. As the leader, I have an obligation to support him, try to do everything I possibly can to do the best, not only for him but for the country."[32] Others, such as Gingrich, were willing to diverge from the White House. According to one senior Republican: "There are those Republicans, like myself, for whom being a Member of Congress is an end in itself. Others see their role as supporting the president and the party; they adopt an our-president-right-or-wrong attitude." Said a veteran leadership aide: "Newt wants to tear down the walls and scream in the president's face. Bob Michel wants his epitaph to read: 'He was a good soldier.' "

During the 1990 budget fight, the "good soldiers" took a beating. After open rebellion in the ranks, Bush aides used heavy-handed tactics to secure Republican support. According to one news account, chief of staff John Sununu told House Republicans: "This is the president's budget and when he comes to your district to campaign for you he's going to look you in the eye and say why aren't you supporting this?"[33] Carl Pursell (R-Michigan), who had often worked with Democrats on budget issues, angrily told Sununu to stop making threats. Sununu's outburst alienated many other House Republicans. Only seventy-one supported the package, compared with 105 who joined a majority of House Democrats to oppose it. Gingrich led the charge against the plan, while Michel supported Bush.

After a budget finally passed, ill will remained both within the House GOP and between it and the White House. Dick Armey (R-Texas), who had authored the antitax conference resolution, was still hitting the administration a year later: "President Bush is dangerously out of touch with the American public. Instead of listening to the elected people in his party most in touch with the average voter—House Republicans—he remains cloistered with aides who avoid action and favor blaming others for the nation's economic, and their boss's consequent political, woes."[34]

Although the Democratic presidential victory in 1992 constituted bad news for the GOP in general, it did the House Republicans a favor by removing a key source of internal division. Some Republicans might vote with the Clinton administration from time to time, but none would feel the same sense of obligation they had when Republicans held the White House. Said Bob Michel: "I've got the best conservative voting record on our side of the aisle, except for a few situations where in the past 12 years I've been the point man in the House for the [Republican] administration. I can go back to voting the strict conservative line that's always been mine from the beginning."[35]

Early in the Clinton term, Armey wrote in a *Washington Times* op-ed: "In 100 days, the Clinton administration has done what conventional wisdom suggested could not be done in 100 years: made the Republican Party whole again. Rather than render us irrelevant, they've revitalized our movement." In a nutshell, "[t]he simple, two-word answer to many of our [GOP] problems is: Bill Clinton."[36]

National Strategy vs. Local Strategy

As mentioned in the previous chapter, some Republicans have sought to attack the Democrats on national issues. During the 1980s, the "nationalizers" had an effect on the National Republican Congressional Committee (NRCC), which put a great deal of money into "generic" party advertising that stressed "wedge" issues. According to a prominent adherent of this school: "I favor a national confrontational approach for the sake of the country, and not just to help House Republicans overcome their permanent minority status. Too often, House elections are devoid of serious issue campaigning. I'm interested in an issues campaign for the good of the country."

Other Republicans have argued for a district-by-district approach. Before his 1992 defeat, Mickey Edwards said: "We have campaigned totally wrong for years. . . . If the Republican Congressional committee had in the future continued to do what we've done in the past—talking about silver bullets, talking about the great national themes, about Jim Wright—we'd never be a majority of anything."[37] In a 1991 memorandum to the House GOP leadership, Edwards said, "*the key to victory is diversity in candidate selection and decentralization of campaign issue selection*" (emphasis in original).

According to a top Democratic leadership aide, the GOP suffered from its failure to heed Edwards: "The House Republicans have never really tried the district-by-district approach, which is our approach, and why we're successful. Instead, they've tried to throw the long bomb, and the long bomb is a very low percentage play."

A top Republican aide disagreed vehemently, insisting that the notion that "all politics is local" is the "great lie of American politics. Rather, all politics of the Democrats is local, while all Republican politics is national. . . . If we make an issue conservative versus liberal, we crush them." This staffer acknowledged that "in reality, politics is a little of both: national and local." But he went on to argue that Republicans cannot afford to play the Democrats' game. If an election race is based on who is going to give more to constituent groups, he maintained, Republicans lose. His comments were reminiscent of Democrat Charlie Stenholm's legendary Christmas-party taunt of Santa-clad Health and Human Services Secretary Republican Louis Sullivan: "I feel sorry for you, Santa. You have only one day every year to be Santa Claus . . . I have 365 days."

On assuming the co-chairmanship at NRCC, Ed Rollins tried the district-by-district approach. He said that as a Reaganite, he knew about revolutions, but "they are president-driven, not whip-driven."[38] Gingrich resented such comments, and tried to have Rollins fired. Jerry Lewis defended Rollins: "Every person who's a member of Congress and has had success politically knows a certain amount about politics. It's like all of us think we know a lot about education because we vote on a bill. Hopefully over time we learn it's better not to tell our kids' teachers what to do or our kids' principals how to run a school."[39]

In the 1990 elections, Republicans suffered a net loss of nine seats; and perhaps more important, nineteen incumbents won their lowest winning percentages ever. Frustrated by this showing and embittered with intraparty bickering, Rollins quit.

The election marked a dark victory for the district-by-district approach. Among the GOP incumbents who barely squeaked by was Gingrich. "When I won by 970 votes, I stopped to rethink everything," he said a few months later. "If we were so damned smart, why aren't we a majority?"[40] Gingrich embraced a greater party emphasis on grass-roots campaigning, and the rift with Edwards appeared to heal.

A year later, however, the consensus began to fray as some Republicans sought to make a national issue out of the House Bank scandals. Gingrich joined with a group of freshmen, the "Gang of Seven," to blame the Democrats for the procedures that had allowed hundreds of members to make multiple overdrafts at the bank. Although some Democratic overdrafters lost reelection, many others came from districts that the GOP could not win. Meanwhile, the issue hurt a number of Republicans in 1992. Edwards (386 overdrafts) lost his primary, and Gingrich (twenty-two overdrafts) was nearly upset by his primary challenger and had to spend huge sums to win the general election.

Vin Weber decided to retire, in part because he recoiled from the prospect of a reelection campaign that would inevitably focus on his own overdrafts. In the summer of 1992, he said that it was fine for Republican challengers to talk about overdrafts and pay raises, but that such matters were no substitute for a strong set of national policy issues.

Liberals and Democrats always have the advantage when Republicans lack a coherent national agenda. This is because Democrats instinctively know what to stand for on local issues that voters care about. The Democratic answer is: "We can solve all these problems. We'll spend more money on the existing federal programs that are designed to meet these needs." . . . Unless we articulate a conservative reform agenda during this campaign, we will undermine our impact on national policy for the next four years.[41]

Unity and Disunity

Because of these divisions, Republicans have often had a hard time closing ranks for the sake of politics or policy. Floor votes supply only a partial glimpse of the House GOP's family feuds, but they do quantify at least one aspect of the House GOP's challenge.

The 1980s saw a rise in average party unity scores for both parties, as Democrats became more liberal and Republicans more conservative. The Democrats, however, had a sharper increase. In every year between 1982 and 1992, their average party unity score exceeded the Republicans'.[42] The gap becomes clearer when one looks at *ranges* instead of *averages*. In 1991 and 1992, Democrats were much more likely than Republicans to score 90 or better, and much less likely to score 79 or less (Table 2-3).

In 1993, House Republicans showed extraordinary unity in *opposing* President Clinton's economic legislation: not one voted for the administration's budget resolution or reconciliation bill. They had less unity,

Table 2-3
Party Unity Scores of Republicans and Democrats
in the U.S. House, 1991 and 1992

	1991		1992	
	Republicans	Democrats	Republicans	Democrats
90–100	31% (52)	48% (128)	39% (64)	52% (140)
80–89	33% (55)	28% (74)	29% (48)	27% (71)
70–79	18% (30)	13% (35)	19% (31)	12% (31)
60–69	9% (15)	9% (23)	9% (15)	7% (18)
Under 60	8% (14)	3% (7)	5% (8)	3% (7)

Cell entries represent the number and percentage of Republicans and Democrats who scored within each range.
Source: Authors' calculations from *Congressional Quarterly Weekly Report*, December 28, 1991, 3790–91; December 19, 1992, 3908–9.

however, over what to *support*. Some did not want to propose any alternative, fearing that Democrats would use a Republican budget plan for target practice. Others wanted the GOP to offer a "balanced package" that included some tax increases.[43] Eventually John Kasich won over the bulk of the Conference with his $500 billion package of spending cuts without tax increases. Though 132 Republicans supported the Kasich package, forty-one voted against it.

In addition to factional divisions,the "rules of the game" also help explain the GOP's disadvantage. Since the early 1980s, the Democrats have increasingly used restrictive rules to structure floor debates. To be sure, many restrictive rules have served merely to lubricate House business, but many others have had partisan purposes. By carefully deciding which amendments could reach the floor and which would languish, a majority can ensure that roll calls maximize its own unity and disrupt the minority.

Party discipline also distinguishes Republicans from Democrats. Control of the House endows the Democrats with disciplinary tools that Republicans lack, such as withholding committee chairmanships or crafting of special rules that impede the passage of a bill. The Democrats sharpen their tools through practice. According to Republican Henry Hyde of Illinois, Democratic leaders pressed their ranks to oppose a White House–backed alternative to the Civil Rights Bill of 1990, threatening at least one member with the loss of a chairmanship. "The arm-twisting was almost legendary," he said. "It's hard to argue with success, but I'm glad I'm a Republican. They [Democrats] can't take away my bathroom privileges or my committee assignments."[44]

Gerald Solomon of New York, ranking Republican on the Rules Committee, faulted his own side: "The House Republicans are partly to blame for failing to articulate our differences with the House Democrats. And the House Republican leadership is partly to blame for not maintaining party discipline. Frankly, the Democrats are better at whipping their membership." Added a moderate midwesterner: "Republicans are by nature individuals and not good at working as a team."

As the next chapter shows, the House GOP's struggle to overcome this frustrating disunity has left its mark on the structure, composition, and behavior of the House Republican leadership.

Notes

1. Phil Duncan, "Looking Beyond Gridlock," *The New Congress*, supplement to *Congressional Quarterly Weekly Report*, January 16, 1993, 12. For an

analysis of House Republican factions, see Douglas L. Koopman, "The House Divided: House Republican Party Factions Revealed in the 1989 Gingrich-Madigan Whip Race" (paper presented at the annual meeting of the Midwest Political Science Association, Chicago, April 18–20, 1991).

2. "Many of the differences between Republicans and Democrats in the U.S. Congress can be explained by the relatively heterogeneous constituency of the Democratic party and the relatively homogeneous constituency of the congressional Republicans." David W. Brady and Charles W. Bullock III, "Party and Faction," in *Handbook of Legislative Research*, ed. Gerhard Loewenberg, Samuel C. Patterson, and Malcolm E. Jewell (Cambridge, Mass.: Harvard University Press, 1985), 140.

3. *The Federalist*, ed. Jacob E. Cooke (1961; reprint, Middletown, Conn.: Wesleyan University Press, 1982), number 10, pp. 58–59. Madison applied the term *faction* not just to any interest, but only to one driven by some impulse or passion "adverse to the rights of other citizens, or to the permanent and aggregate interests of the community (number 10, p. 57). Following contemporary usage, however, we employ the term more broadly.

4. Nicol C. Rae, *The Decline and Fall of the Liberal Republicans From 1952 to the Present* (New York: Oxford University Press, 1989), 158–63. See also Charles O. Jones, "The Voters Say Yes: The 1984 Congressional Elections," in *Election 84: Landslide Without a Mandate?*, ed. Ellis Sandoz and Cecil V. Crabb (New York: New American Library/Mentor Books, 1985), 99–101.

5. David W. Rohde, *Parties and Leaders in the Postreform House* (Chicago: University of Chicago Press, 1991), 124.

6. Burdett Loomis makes a similar point about Democrats in *The New American Politician: Ambition, Entrepreneurship, and the Changing Face of Political Life*, paperback ed. (New York: Basic, 1990), 47.

7. Calculated from seniority data in: Phil Duncan, ed. *Politics in America 1994: The 103rd Congress* (Washington, D.C.: CQ Press, 1993), 1737–38. Strictly speaking, those elected in 1980 did serve for a few weeks under Jimmy Carter, but we do not count them here.

8. Quoted in Timothy J. Burger, "Bob Michel Defends Statement Labeling Frosh as 'Hard-Line,' " *Roll Call*, August 16, 1993, 1.

9. Quoted in "Politics '93: Richard Pombo," *Human Events*, August 7, 1993, 16.

10. Peter Overby, "White-Picket Welfare," *Common Cause Magazine*, Fall 1993, 21–26.

11. Quoted in Susan F. Rasky, "Tax Specter Shadows a GOP Leader," *New York Times*, May 14, 1990, A12.

12. Quoted in Duncan, *Politics in America 1994*, 1310.

13. Quoted in Timothy J. Burger, "Will Gingrich's Allies Attempt Coup Against Ranking Members Like They Did in 1992?" *Roll Call*, November 1, 1993, 38.

14. Quoted in Michael Barone and Grant Ujifusa, *The Almanac of American Politics 1994* (Washington: Times Mirror/National Journal, 1993), 1122.

15. Quoted in Timothy J. Burger, "Gingrich's Failed Bid to Remove Thomas Part of a Larger Effort," *Roll Call*, December 15, 1992, 19.

16. Quoted in Richard E. Cohen, "Minority Blues," *National Journal*, May 9, 1987, 1156.

17. Quoted in Steven V. Roberts, "The 92 Group: Moderate Republicans Lay Plans," *New York Times*, May 15, 1985, B12.

18. Mickey Edwards, "A Revolution? Now? Against What?" *Washington Post*, December 2, 1984, D8.

19. Quoted in Paul Barton, "Boehner Emerging in House as GOP Leadership Material," Gannett News Service, August 7, 1993.

20. Quoted in Bill McKenzie, "A Conversation With Newt Gingrich," *Ripon Forum*, May 1989, 4.

21. Sula P. Richardson, *Caucuses and Legislative Service Organizations of the 102nd Congress: An Informational Directory* (Washington, D.C.: Library of Congress/Congressional Research Service, 1992), 6.

22. Richard E. Cohen and William Schneider, "Partisan Polarization," *National Journal*, January 18, 1992, 132.

23. Quoted in Merrill Hartson, "GOP Announces Legislative Agenda for 'Choice' But No Abortion Mention," Associated Press, February 7, 1990.

24. *Congressional Record*, daily ed., October 1, 1991, H7148. Republican Tom Campbell was actually serving his second term.

25. *Congressional Record*, daily ed., October 2, 1991, H7204.

26. *Congressional Quarterly Weekly Report*, March 27, 1993, 792.

27. *Congressional Quarterly Weekly Report*, July 3, 1993, 1776.

28. Quoted in Tom Kenworthy and Guy Gugliotta, "Upbeat House GOP Encounters Old Divisions," *Washington Post*, March 16, 1991, A10.

29. Quoted in Ronald Powers, "Congressman Solomon to Seek House Republican Leadership Post," Associated Press, October 4, 1993.

30. Quoted in Robert W. Merry, "Weber Seeks to Reshape GOP," *Wall Street Journal*, December 27, 1984, 36.

31. Quoted in Allan Ryskind and John Gizzi, "Weber's Advice to George Bush," *Human Events*, April 25, 1992, 4.

32. Quoted in Christopher Madison, "Pint-Sized Elephant," *National Journal*, January 19, 1991, 132.

33. Quoted in Eli Teiber and Fredric Dicker, "GOPers See Red on Budget Threats," *New York Post*, October 2, 1990, 2.

34. Dick Armey, "Down With the Palace Guard," *New York Times*, November 26, 1991, A19.

35. Quoted in Kenneth J. Cooper, "With More Conservative Cast, House GOP Vows 'Militant' Approach," *Washington Post*, December 14, 1992, A9.

36. Dick Armey, "GOP Revived With 100 Opportunities," *Washington Times*, April 29, 1993, G4.

37. Quoted in Kim Mattingly, "Republicans Talk Strategy and Ways to Regain Control of House in 1992," *Roll Call*, March 1, 1990, 18.

38. Quoted in Don Phillips and Ann Devroy, "Gingrich Wanted Rollins Fired in GOP Strategy Feud," *Washington Post*, November 30, 1989, A4.

39. Quoted in Bill Whalen, "Party Animal," *Campaigns and Elections*, November 1990, 31.

40. Quoted in Jackie Calmes, "In an About-Face, Gingrich Becomes an Apostle of Grass-Roots Politics, Averting Clashes in GOP," *Wall Street Journal*, March 27, 1991, A16.

41. Vin Weber, "No Mandate for Leadership: The Idea Vacuum in the GOP," *Policy Review* 61 (Summer 1992): 35.

42. Norman J. Ornstein, Thomas E. Mann, and Michael J. Malbin, *Vital Statistics on Congress 1993-1994* (Washington, D.C.: CQ Press, 1994), 202.

43. Major Garrett, "GOP Feuds Over Alternative," *Washington Times*, March 17, 1993, A7.

44. Quoted in Chris Harvey, "Democrats Show Muscle in Blitzing Civil Rights Alternative," *Washington Times*, August 6, 1990, A5.

Chapter 3

Leadership Structure

In *Reflections on the Revolution in France*, Edmund Burke looked at the French National Assembly to draw a broader lesson about lawmaking: "In all bodies, those who will lead, must also, in a considerable degree, follow. They must conform their propositions to the taste, talent, and disposition of those they wish to conduct. . . ."[1] In Burke's tradition, many scholars have described congressional leadership as a form of followership, in which leaders swim with tides they cannot control. Individual skills have less influence than institutional context: to understand leadership, look to the members before the leaders.[2]

This point of view has merit. Taken too far, however, it can lead to a blinkered perspective that ignores key elements of congressional life. House Republicans act as if leaders mattered. In recent years, they have argued at length about the leadership structure, and their internal elections have sometimes turned into political knife fights.

Dick Cheney (R-Wyoming), who rose from Policy Committee chair to whip during the 1980s, did not cause any GOP bloodshed. His colleagues, including Robert Michel and Newt Gingrich, were willing to defer to his judgment because they admired his intellect and respected his experience as President Gerald Ford's chief of staff. Cheney, who first came to Washington as a Congressional Fellow of the American Political Science Association, has analyzed the significance of individual leaders. *Kings of the Hill*, a 1983 book he coauthored with his wife Lynne Cheney, argues that leaders can make a difference by molding their environment: "No sooner do we think we've reached the resolution of the play than a creative leader steps onstage, picks up plot threads we had barely noticed, and uses them to begin a new act."[3]

Baroque Architecture

The Posts

From the late 1940s until the mid-1980s, House Republicans created a number of new leadership positions and party organizations. In this decentralized structure, the Republican Leader had little power, but in the late 1980s, the members took tentative steps to give the position more authority. Because the House Republican leadership has received little attention in the scholarly literature, we should pause at this point to take a quick overview of the leadership offices.

The House Republicans elect eight leaders:

Republican Leader. Believing that the term "Minority Leader" suggested resignation to minority status, Robert Michel started his time in the job by insisting on the title of "Republican Leader."[4] Whatever the title, the position carries far less weight than the Speakership. The Republican Leader has little say about the floor calendar or the administration of the chamber. For instance, the Leader controls just one small meeting room, H-227 Capitol. If Republicans need a larger place to meet, they must take what the majority gives them.

To wield real influence with their rank-and-file members, party leaders need power over committee assignments. House Speakers gained strength when they got the power to name a large fraction of the Steering and Policy Committee, which decides Democratic assignments. On the Republican side, the power to recommend assignments lies with the party's Committee on Committees, which consists of: the Leader; the whip; and representatives elected by large states, groups of small states, and the two most recent incoming classes. While chairing the Committee, the Leader does not name any of its other members and can cast only a fraction of its weighted vote.

Whip. Like whips in other legislative bodies, the House Republican whip traffics in legislative information and tries to win votes for the party's positions. Unlike the majority whip, who helps set the legislative agenda, the minority whip must react to it. In the words of one GOP whip staffer, "Our job comes late in the game."

On becoming whip in 1989, Gingrich named two chief deputy whips: one for traditional legislative work on the House floor, and one for strategy and special projects. The latter post was a Gingrich innovation. Instead of monitoring amendments and rounding up votes, the second chief deputy whip helped develop policy proposals and organized special events, such as a 1990 round-the-clock special order on crime.

Conference Chair. In 1911, Republicans officially changed the name of their caucus to the Republican Conference in order to escape the connotation of a "caucus" as a backroom organization that could bind its members' votes.[5] Despite the difference in titles, the Republican Conference chairman has duties similar to those of the Democratic Caucus chairman: arranging meetings of all the party members, winning political support for party positions, developing legislation, and spreading information on policy and politics. The Conference publishes *Legislative Digest*, a weekly publication that analyzes bills before the House. In recent years, the Conference has also set up an electronic bulletin board providing GOP members and staff with meeting announcements, leadership statements, personnel notices, and other useful items.

In the 101st Congress, Conference Chairman Jerry Lewis (R-California) established a "board of directors" to advise him on legislative management and electoral politics. Deliberately forgoing press attention, Lewis worked behind the scenes to help members exchange political intelligence. Lewis's successor, Dick Armey (R-Texas) promised even more extensive member services and a more public fight against the Democrats. In 1993, he announced plans for "a rapid response truth squad" consisting of House GOP policy experts. Said Armey's top aide: "The idea is simply lifted right out of the Clinton/ Gore campaign playbook. When President Clinton comes out with a project, or the Democratic leaders offer a program, we want to be able to get our response out and picked up by the media within an hour."[6] When Clinton issued his health-care reform proposal, the Conference attacked by releasing an organization chart purporting to show the plan's mind-numbing complexity. The chart appeared in a number of publications, including the *Wall Street Journal* and Rush Limbaugh's newsletter.[7]

Policy Committee Chair. The House Republican Policy Committee has thirty-five members: the elected House Republican leaders and the freshman leadership representative; the ranking GOP members of Appropriations, Budget, Rules, and Ways and Means; eight regional representatives; ten at-large members chosen by the Republican Leader; and four members from the two most recent classes. The Policy Committee's main formal duty is to issue statements on matters before the House. In the fall of 1993, for example, it adopted a statement on crime:

> What the House Democrats did this week was a crime. They used every trick in their legislative book to prevent meaningful votes on tough measures to restore safety to our streets and security to our homes. . . . Then they brought to the floor—under suspension of the rules—five mini-bills, four of them grant programs without any realistic source of funding, all sidestepping the crucial issues in the fight against crime. . . . So while the country bleeds, the House is gagged. While the public lives in fear, House Democrats fear to vote in public.[8]

The Policy Committee also provides Republicans with closed-door issue discussions that are more structured than cloakroom bull sessions and more manageable than meetings of the full Conference.[9]

Research Committee Chair. The Research Committee is perhaps the least-known part of the formal leadership. Sometimes, even Republican members confuse it with the Policy Committee or the Republican Study Committee. The Research Committee puts out issue papers and organizes publicity events for members. The Committee's work is conducted both by its core staff and by member task forces, which have concentrated on issues ranging from acid rain to the Baltic States. These task forces seldom have an immediate impact on legislation, but their reports and events occasionally catch the eye of the press or the relevant policy community.

Vice Chair and **Secretary.** The vice chair and secretary of the Conference serve as ministers without portfolio. The vice chair presides over meetings in the chairman's absence; otherwise, these offices carry few defined duties. While the Leader, whip, Policy chair, and Research chair all get extra leadership staff, these two positions carry none. "In a sense, all leaders are equal," said one vice chairman, referring to the collegiality among the members of the leadership. But most House Republicans see these as junior positions whose main value lies in giving their occupants a springboard for higher leadership office.

Chair of the National Republican Congressional Committee (NRCC). This position differs from the others in that much of its work takes place off the Capitol grounds. NRCC, headquartered near the Cannon House Office Building, provides campaign money and services for GOP House candidates. Unlike his Democratic counterparts, longtime

NRCC Chair Guy Vander Jagt (R-Michigan) opted to work on the outside, leaving floor and committee maneuvers to the other leaders. The Vander Jagt years, therefore, saw surprisingly little coordination between the House Republicans' electoral strategies and their governing strategies. Vander Jagt's successor, Bill Paxon (R-New York) began his tenure by trying to launch a closer working relationship with the House Republican Conference.[11]

Other Leaders. In addition to these eight positions, Conference rules define the party leadership to include the ranking Republicans on the Committees on Appropriations, Budget, Rules, and Ways and Means. And in the 103d Congress, an additional rules change made a representative of the freshman class a member of the leadership.

Why So Many Leaders?

A glance at the leadership structure reveals duplication and overlap. The whip and the chairs of Conference, Policy, and Research all supply information to the members. Although Research is not charged with setting policy, the distinction between analysis and advocacy can fade, so the Research and Policy chairs may often have to work out turf conflicts. The Democrats also have an elaborate leadership structure.[12] But while control of the House gives the Democrats plenty of power to allot among their leaders, Republicans have far less power to spare. Why do they have so many offices when the occupants can achieve so little?

Electoral setbacks have sometimes prompted organizational shuffling. The minority may react to defeat by changing the one thing it does control: its own organization. After Republicans lost the majority in 1948—in a campaign where they let Truman paint them as "the do-nothing Congress"—they turned their wheezing Steering Committee into the Policy Committee.[13] But under the chairmanship of Republican Leader Joseph Martin, the new committee dawdled. After the GOP lost forty-eight seats in 1958, younger members ousted Martin from the leadership and the party named a separate chairman of the Policy Committee. In the wake of the 1964 Democratic landslide, they replaced Republican Leader Charles Halleck (R-Indiana) with Gerald Ford (R-Michigan), who set up the Committee on Research and Planning, later the Research Committee.[14] No similar upheaval followed the losses of 1974 and 1982. Both times, the Leader was new and thus hard to blame. Instead of seeking scapegoats, the members cited external causes: Watergate in 1974, the recession in 1982.

Creating leadership jobs and appointive party posts is also one of the few ways in which the minority leadership can reward old friends, attract new supporters, or sidestep internal conflicts. In 1965, Gerald Ford wanted the Policy chair for Charles Goodell (R-New York), who had helped Ford win the Leadership. But rather than tangle with conservatives who sought the job for John Rhodes (R-Arizona), Ford established the Research post for Goodell.[15] Similarly, Gingrich created the second chief deputy whip's job for Steve Gunderson (R-Wisconsin), who had brought crucial votes to Gingrich in his race for whip.

This discussion raises the question of why House Republicans want leadership and party posts in the first place. One reason is that minority status deprives them of legislative chairs, a big outlet for ambition.[16] A freshman Democrat can look forward to swinging a gavel within a few years: in 1981, most of the remaining Democrats of the 1974 class were already chairing a subcommittee. By contrast, no sitting House Republican has ever chaired a committee or subcommittee; and as of the early 1990s, few expected to do so. The post of "ranking member" makes a poor substitute.

For a Republican craving prestige, a party post supplies the best available substitute for the legislative power enjoyed by Democrats. The GOP's elected leaders are sometimes excluded from key negotiations, but they do have more contact with the president and majority's leadership than other Republicans.

An appointed post, while carrying less prestige than an elected leadership position, can give a member a feeling of participation. "You have all these other members looking for something to do," said a leadership aide in 1987, "You have them join task forces and that's how they try to be relevant." The posts may also have minor electoral benefits. In 1986, Henson Moore (R-Louisiana) wanted black votes in his U.S. Senate race; the Research Committee created for Moore a task force on minority opportunity. More generally, members can use party posts to enhance their prestige back home: they can put the title on letterhead and discuss their leadership activities in newsletters.

Drawbacks of Dispersal

The dispersal of leadership has costs. One problem, "title inflation," is suggested by this item from *Roll Call*:

During debate on the RTC rule, Rep. David Dreier (R-Calif.) was introducing Republican Members by referring to their leadership titles, such as the "chairman of the Republican Research Committee" or "the distinguished chairman of the Republican Study Committee." It seemed like every House Republican had a title. After Dreier introduced Rep. Vin Weber (R-Minn.) as "the distinguished secretary of the Republican Conference and a member of the Appropriations Committee," Democrats let out a loud, sarcastic "Oooooohhh." That prompted a grinning Speaker Pro Tem Steny Hoyer (D-Md.) to warn, "The Chair would remind the Members to be respectful of these titles."[17]

Much more significant was the scant unity of effort among leadership offices during the late 1980s and early 1990s. In 1992, a leadership aide made an offhand but striking comment about NRCC: "I don't know what they do over there."

When a legislative minority has many officers unaccountable to its Leader, it may lose its meager influence in a jumble of voices. A Leader with little internal authority has a hard time keeping members from abandoning party issue positions for separate deals with outside interests or the majority party. During the 1980s, the increasingly powerful Democratic leadership team daunted the House Republicans. Contrary to the conventional image of fractious Democrats and disciplined Republicans, many members of the minority party saw the Democrats as the A-Team and themselves as F-Troop.

House Democrats, in giving more power to their leadership, sought in part to make it more effective against Republican presidents. Ironically, by the mid-1980s, congressional GOP loyalists also wanted to strengthen *their* leadership for conflicts with a Republican White House. And even those who normally sided with the White House often found their loyalty strained. Said Cheney: "We have found an institutional conflict here between what the President wants to do and what we want to do. The President needs Democratic votes to pass his programs. We want confrontation, not cooperation."[18] In interviews during the late 1980s and early 1990s, members and staff repeatedly said that the White House slighted House Republicans. Said one leadership aide:

Things soured when Reagan got comfortable. They saw an ultraviolet mandate that covered everything in a White House glow. White House meetings [with the GOP leadership] were and, to some extent, still are either for the White House to dictate something, or for the leaders to play standup comedians for the camera. And a few times, Michel has declined invitations.

In dealings with both the White House and House Democrats, the dispersed leadership structure left Michel with a weak hand. In 1985 and 1986, tax reform politics cast a harsh light onto the structure's frailties.

Tax Reform and Republican Leadership

In 1985, President Ronald Reagan made tax reform his top domestic priority. Throughout the summer and fall, Ways and Means chairman Dan Rostenkowski (D-Illinois) worked with committee Democrats—and a few Republicans—to devise a tax bill bearing Rostenkowski's own stamp. As the committee was finishing its work, House Republicans voiced growing opposition. Some "district guys" balked at the bill because it would hurt constituents or supporters. Young conservatives thought it was insufficiently "pro-growth and pro-family."[19] And most important, nearly all Republicans resented the way White House aides had handled the issue. Said Gingrich: "They thought they could work for six months with Rostenkowski and then six hours with us and that would be enough."[20]

On December 11, Republican whip Trent Lott (R-Mississippi) derailed the Rostenkowski proposal. With the support of 90 percent of Republicans and enough Democrats, he engineered the defeat of the rule for considering the bill. Asked whether he had consulted the White House, Lott said: "I would ordinarily have warned them, but I haven't been talking to them much in the last couple of days."[21] Speaker Tip O'Neill observed: "For four or five years, the White House has not been answering their phone calls and [has been] treating them like robots doing their bidding."[22] Another high-ranking Democrat concluded: "Well, they finally found the right combination to get even. They found a bill where their votes made all the difference."[23]

Their victory was ambiguous: they had made a show of strength by stopping their president's bill. And triumph soon turned into yet another frustration as President Reagan switched enough Republican votes to get the bill back onto the floor. On the night of December 17, when the bill came up for a final vote, the House Republicans hit bottom. After the customary voice vote, Speaker O'Neill looked to the GOP side expecting someone to demand a roll call—but no one did. The Speaker waited several long moments, then declared the measure passed. Vin Weber later said: "We screwed up."[24]

While most observers saw the roll-call fiasco as a minor element of the tax-reform story, House Republicans regarded it as a major humiliation. It reminded them of several other ways in which the issue had exposed their party's weaknesses:

- Several Ways and Means "committee guys" had worked closely with Rostenkowski. Other members accused them of selling out the party for their own parochial interests, but fumed that there was no ready means of holding them to account.
- John Duncan, ranking Republican on Ways and Means, was criticized for the Republicans' substitute legislation. Instead of working with the younger conservatives to devise a dramatically different proposal, Duncan's staff did little more than a cut-and-paste job on the Democratic bill.
- Conference Chairman Jack Kemp (R-New York) caught flak for changing tactics after the initial defeat of the rule. Hoping that tax reform would boost his presidential candidacy, he got President Reagan to write him a letter outlining changes he would insist upon from the Senate. Kemp then used the letter to persuade other members to support the bill—even though the Republican Conference had passed a resolution opposing it. Cheney called Kemp "a crack in the armor."[25]

Toward Stronger Leadership

According to a senior leadership aide of the late 1980s, Kemp's shift "ignited a lot of latent frustration, because the COS types can only accomplish things in conference or on the floor. Now the Conference chairman was ignoring the Conference." A number of younger members called for more party discipline, and Republican Leader Michel responded by naming Policy chairman Dick Cheney to head a special task force on rules and procedures.

Based on the Cheney panel's report, the Conference passed a set of rules changes in December 1986. The new rules authorized the Leader to designate "leadership issues," which "require early and ongoing cooperation between the relevant committees and the Leadership as the issue evolves." Ranking Republicans on committees now had an "obligation to ensure that the managerial responsibilities on the Floor of the House of Representatives for each measure on which the Republican Conference has taken a position are managed in accordance with such position." With the tax debate in mind, the Conference also resolved that every GOP leader should "support positions adopted by the Conference, and the resources of the Leadership shall be utilized to support that position."[26]

Recognizing that these changes might seem to lack teeth, the Conference set up another task force to recommend "more effective and disciplined development of Republican policy positions and strategy." The task force had two subcommittees: one on rules, headed by Jan Meyers (R-Kansas); and one on committee assignments, headed by Conference secretary Robert Lagomarsino (R-California). By following the model of the Democratic Caucus rules, the Meyers task force implicitly embraced a more centralized leadership structure.

The Lagomarsino subcommittee brought forth a more concrete change. The Republicans had been making committee assignments through a large Committee on Committees, which delegated most of its work to its Executive Committee on Committees. The leadership had little voice on the Executive Committee, which made decisions by weighted vote. At the start of the 100th Congress, Michel sought an Appropriations seat for Lynn Martin (R-Illinois), but the proposed assignment was shot down in a conflict between members from large and small states. The defeat embarrassed Michel and heightened the image of GOP disarray. The Lagomarsino recommendations, adopted by the Conference in 1988, replaced the old structure with a single Committee on Committees, where both the leader and whip would cast weighted votes. The Leader also gained the power to name new Republican members of the Rules Committee—another echo of the Democratic side, where the corresponding power had gone to the Speaker years earlier. Newt Gingrich called the changes "part of a series of steps House Republicans have been taking to increase Michel's capacity to lead."[27] Now that the Leader had more say over assignments, committee members would have to pay more heed to party positions.

With the rules changes, Michel took a more active role in setting GOP policy. Again emulating the Democrats, he set up leadership task forces to deal with issues such as health care and campaign reform. (These *ad hoc* groups were different from the ongoing Research Committee task forces.) Like Speaker O'Neill's Democratic task forces, these units included members in party activities and helped the party achieve a degree of consensus. Unlike the Democratic groups, the GOP leadership task forces could not set the terms for floor debate, but instead worked to make changes in Democratic legislation.

A puzzle remains. Pressure for reform came from confrontationists such as Newt Gingrich, but the immediate impact was to strengthen Republican Leader Michel, whose statesmanlike style sometimes frustrated those who wanted more partisanship. Why would they want to make Michel more powerful? One answer is they were looking ahead to the post-Michel era, watching trends in the leadership's composition.

Who Leads?

Changes at the Top

Leaders represent party colleagues as well as their geographic constituents, or as one member of the leadership put it: "You're a representative twice." Changes in the House GOP's ideological composition went hand-in-hand with changes in geographical composition. During recent decades, the House Republicans have increasingly come from the South, the West, and the political Right. A glance at leadership rosters (Table 3-1) shows the impact of these changes. Until 1973, every Republican Speaker or Minority Leader had come from the Northeast or Midwest. But when Michigan's Gerald Ford became vice president, his place was taken by a westerner: Policy chairman John Rhodes of Arizona. In addition, the leadership now included two southerners: Research chairman Lou Frey of Florida and Conference secretary Jack Edwards of Alabama.

The regional shift continued in 1980, when Trent Lott of Mississippi became the first Republican whip from the Deep South. In 1987, Jack Kemp of New York resigned the Conference chair to run for president. After the ensuing shuffle of offices, five out of eight elected leadership posts belonged to southerners or westerners, a proportion that remained in place after the next major leadership shift, in 1992.

The ideological change has been just as stark. As late as 1979, the top leadership included a strong liberal: Conference chairman John Anderson (R-Illinois), with a Conservative Coalition support score of just 9 percent. During the next decade, the leadership became solidly conservative. Of the elected leaders of the 1980s, only vice chairman Lynn Martin came in with reputation as a moderate—and even she moved to the right. From 1981 to 1984, her normalized Conservative Coalition support score averaged 70 percent. From 1985 to 1988, it averaged 86 percent. Of the leaders elected in 1992, none had a score for that year below 93 percent.

Table 3-1

House Republican Leadership, 1971–93

	Leader	Whip	Conference	Policy
71–73	Gerald Ford (Mich.)	Leslie Arends (Ill.)	John Anderson (Ill.)	John Rhodes (Ariz.)
73–75	Gerald Ford (Mich.)	Leslie Arends (Ill.)	John Anderson (Ill.)	John Rhodes (Ariz.)
	John Rhodes (Ariz.)			Barber Conable (N.Y.)
75–77	John Rhodes (Ariz.)	Robert Michel (Ill.)	John Anderson (Ill.)	Barber Conable (N.Y.)
77–79	John Rhodes (Ariz.)	Robert Michel (Ill.)	John Anderson (Ill.)	Del Clawson (Cal.)
79–81	John Rhodes (Ariz.)	Robert Michel (Ill.)	John Anderson (Ill.)	Bud Shuster (Penn.)
			Samuel Devine (Ohio)	
81–83	Robert Michel (Ill.)	Trent Lott (Miss.)	Jack Kemp (N.Y.)	Dick Cheney (Wyo.)
83–85	Robert Michel (Ill.)	Trent Lott (Miss.)	Jack Kemp (N.Y.)	Dick Cheney (Wyo.)
85–87	Robert Michel (Ill.)	Trent Lott (Miss.)	Jack Kemp (N.Y.)	Dick Cheney (Wyo.)
87–89	Robert Michel (Ill.)	Trent Lott (Miss.)	Jack Kemp (N.Y.)	Dick Cheney (Wyo.)
			Dick Cheney (Wyo.)	Jerry Lewis (Cal.)
89–91	Robert Michel (Ill.)	Dick Cheney (Wyo.)	Jerry Lewis (Cal.)	Mickey Edwards (Ok.)
		Newt Gingrich (Ga.)		
91–93	Robert Michel (Ill.)	Newt Gingrich (Ga.)	Jerry Lewis (Ca.)	Mickey Edwards (Ok.)
93–	Robert Michel (Ill.)	Newt Gingrich (Ga.)	Dick Armey (Tex.)	Henry Hyde (Ill.)

Table 3-1

House Republican Leadership, 1971–93

	Research	Vice Chair	Secretary	NRCC
71–73	Barber Conable (N.Y.)	Robert Stafford (Vt.) Samuel Devine (Ohio)	Richard Poff (Va.)	Bob Wilson (Cal.)
73–75	Barber Conable (N.Y.) Lou Frey (Fla.)	Samuel Devine (Ohio)	Jack Edwards (Ala.)	Robert Michel (Ill.)
75–77	Lou Frey (Fla.)	Samuel Devine (Ohio)	Jack Edwards (Ala.)	Guy Vander Jagt (Mich.)
77–79	William Frenzel (Mn.)	Samuel Devine (Ohio)	Jack Edwards (Ala.)	Guy Vander Jagt (Mich.)
79–81	Trent Lott (Miss.)	Samuel Devine (Ohio) Jack Edwards (Ala.)	Jack Edwards (Ala.) Clair Burgener (Cal.)	Guy Vander Jagt (Mich.)
81–83	Edward Madigan (Ill.)	Jack Edwards (Ala.)	Clair Burgener (Cal.)	Guy Vander Jagt (Mich.)
83–85	James Martin (N.C.) Jerry Lewis (Cal)	Jack Edwards (Ala.)	R. Lagomarsino (Cal.)	Guy Vander Jagt (Mich.)
85–87	Jerry Lewis (Cal.)	Lynn Martin (Ill.)	R. Lagomarsino (Cal.)	Guy Vander Jagt (Mich.)
87–89	Jerry Lewis (Cal.) Mickey Edwards (Ok.)	Lynn Martin (Ill.)	R. Lagomarsino (Cal.)	Guy Vander Jagt (Mich.)
89–91	Duncan Hunter (Cal.)	Bill McCollum (Fla.)	Vin Weber (Mn.)	Guy Vander Jagt (Mich.)
91–93	Duncan Hunter (Cal.)	Bill McCollum (Fla.)	Vin Weber (Mn.)	Guy Vander Jagt (Mich.)
93–	Duncan Hunter (Cal.)	Bill McCollum (Fla.)	Tom DeLay (Tex.)	Bill Paxon (N.Y.)

Contested Leadership Elections

Because the House Republicans choose their leaders by secret ballot, the only public data on contested leadership elections consist of overall vote totals. These numbers, however crude they may be, do cast light on the changing character of the House Republican Conference (Table 3-2). In 1979, when John Anderson left the Conference chair to run for president, younger members disdained the "responsible partner" candidate, Samuel Devine (R-Ohio), in favor of Henry Hyde (R-Illinois). Although Hyde belonged to the World War II generation, his legislation to ban abortion funding showed that he was no stranger to "wedge" issues. He argued with eloquence in floor debates and television appearances. Hyde lost, but his strong showing suggested that the bombthrowers were gathering momentum.

In late 1980, when the Republicans were organizing for the next Congress, Robert Walker (R-Pennsylvania) became the first of the future COS members to seek a leadership post. He won a fair number of votes, but the Conference still drew back from confrontationism, as the responsible partners continued to enjoy an apparent majority. Reporting on the five 1980 leadership contests, *National Journal* remarked: "In each case, the winner has shown a greater propensity to work with Democrats on legislative issues."[28]

The mid-1980s saw little turnover in the leadership. Then, in 1987, Kemp followed Anderson's precedent by resigning the Conference chairmanship to run for president. Without opposition, Cheney moved from Policy to Conference. The resulting vacancy at Policy prompted a contest between Research chairman Jerry Lewis and COS leader Duncan Hunter (R-California). Besides belonging to the leadership, Lewis sat on Appropriations and influenced committee assignments as the California representative on the Committee on Committees. These posts had enabled him to put out many chits among GOP members. As a westerner, a member of the post–World War II generation, and an economic conservative, Lewis stood on the right side of several of the Conference's divides. These advantages, together with his genial personality, should have meant easy victory. But the more-confrontational Hunter enjoyed intense support from bombthrowers. Hunter came within a few votes of victory, which indicated that the bombthrowers were nearing a breakthrough. And in the Conference's organizing session in late 1988, Hunter and two other COS members (Weber and McCollum) won leadership posts by wide margins.

A few months later, Cheney (who had now become whip) left the

Table 3-2
Contested Elections for House GOP Leadership Posts, 1978–92

Date	Office	Winner	Vote	Loser
12-04-78	Conf. Chair	Anderson (Ill.)	87–55	Kindness (Ohio)
12-04-78	Policy	Shuster (Penn.)	80–55	Frenzel (Mn.)
12-04-78	Research	Lott (Miss.)	NA	*
06-20-79	Conf. Chair	Devine (Ohio)	75–72	Hyde (Ill.)
06-20-79	Secretary	Burgener (Cal.)	84–57	Bauman (Md.)
12-08-80	Leader	Michel (Ill.)	103–87	Vander Jagt (Mich.)
12-08-80	Whip	Lott (Miss.)	96–90	Shuster (Penn.)
12-08-80	Conf. Chair	Kemp (N.Y.)	107–77	Rousselot (Cal.)
12-08-80	Policy	Cheney (Wyo.)	99–68	Holt (Md.)
12-08-80	Research	Madigan (Ill.)	93–74	Walker (Penn.)
11-02-83	Research	Lewis (Cal.)	78–47	Coleman (Mo.)**
06-04-87	Policy	Lewis (Cal.)	88–82	Hunter (Cal.)
06-04-87	Research	Edwards (Ok.)	93–71	Bartlett (Tex.)
12-05-88	Conf. Chair	Lewis (Cal.)	85–82	Martin (Ill.)
12-05-88	Research	Hunter (Cal.)	100–65	Bartlett (Tex.)
12-05-88	Vice Chair	McCollum (Fla.)	110–50	Lagomarsino (Cal.)
12-05-88	Secretary	Weber (Mn.)	82–61	McDade (Penn.)***
03-02-89	Whip	Gingrich (Ga.)	87–85	Madigan (Ill.)
12-03-90	Conf. Chair	Lewis (Cal.)	98–64	Pursell (Mich.)
12-03-90	NRCC	Vander Jagt (Mich.)	98–66	Sundquist (Tenn.)
12-07-92	Conf. Chair	Armey (Tex.)	88–84	Lewis (Cal.)
12-08-92	Vice Chair	McCollum (Fla.)	93–70	Johnson (Conn.)
12-08-92	Secretary	DeLay (Tex.)	95–71	Gradison (Ohio)

When more than one ballot was required, results of final ballot are shown.
*On the first ballot, Lott won a majority against Lawrence Coughlin (Penn.) and Willis Gradison (Ohio), but the Conference did not announce the tally.
**Lynn Martin (Ill.) received 30 votes.
***Jan Meyers (Kan.) received 17 votes.
Sources: *Congressional Quarterly Weekly Report*, *National Journal*, *New York Times*, *Roll Call*, *Washington Post*, various years.

House to become Defense Secretary, and the race to succeed him attracted Gingrich and Edward Madigan of Illinois. In this contest, factional lines crossed and blurred. Madigan, a close ally of Michel, was a responsible partner with a fairly conservative voting record. As the 1990 *Almanac of American Politics* put it: "Madigan campaigned as a man who knows how to count votes, how to influence colleagues, and how to work with Democrats. . . ."[29] Madigan could count on strong support from "district guys" and "committee guys." He also had support from some "old right" conservatives, as his campaign manager was Tom DeLay of Texas.

Gingrich, conversely, augmented his core of bombthrowers with a number of political moderates and responsible partners who applauded his enthusiasm for new ideas. After the vote, he said: "I carried New England by seven to three; I was nominated by Bill Frenzel [R-Minnesota]; Olympia Snowe [R-Maine] seconded my nomination; and others like Steve Gunderson and Claudine Schneider [R-Rhode Island] played major roles. So I regard my election as a coalition victory for activists of all the ideological views of the Republican Party."[30] Gingrich also had lucky timing: his fight against Speaker Jim Wright got a warm reception even among conciliatory Republicans, who often seethed at Wright's harsh methods.

Gingrich, however, carried some heavy baggage. His affection for innovation alienated some of the "old-right" conservatives, who mounted an abortive drive to get Henry Hyde into the race.[31] And his forceful, sometimes abrasive, personality surely cost him some support. So even though Hunter, McCollum, and Weber had won leadership posts by wide margins, Gingrich won by a vote of 87-85.

The next contested leadership races took place after the disappointing election of 1990. Having lost seats in the previous two elections, House Republicans thought they had nowhere to go but up—yet they still lost more seats. Much of their dissatisfaction turned to NRCC chair Guy Vander Jagt. His challenger, Don Sundquist of Tennessee, raised questions about NRCC staff, but Sundquist himself had to rebut accusations that the Bush White House had sponsored his candidacy. Vander Jagt had solidified his base by cultivating bombthrowers and conservatives. He also quelled much of the dismay by promising to address specific problems with NRCC operations. According to one anonymous six-term Republican: "There is a big feeling that we just have to get a broom in there and sweep the place out. But there are others who feel a bloodletting is not what we need."[32] Vander Jagt beat Sundquist 98-66.

Carl Pursell, the responsible partner who had taken on John Sununu during the 1990 budget battle, meanwhile challenged Jerry Lewis for the chair of the House Republican Conference. Backed by Gingrich, Pursell argued that he would be more aggressive than Lewis in defending the GOP conference against both the Democrats and the White

House. Lewis had supported Bush throughout the budget debate, and some observers thought that the White House connection might handicap him, as it was hobbling Sundquist. But unlike Duncan Hunter, Pursell could not chip at Lewis's support from the right: Lewis's 1990 Conservative Coalition score was 92, compared with Pursell's 78. Pursell had voted for federal funding of abortion, while Lewis had voted against it. Many of the conservatives, even some bombthrowers, probably deemed Lewis more acceptable than the moderate Pursell. At the same time, many moderates and responsible partners had no particular gripe with Lewis, who had done them many practical favors. Lewis defeated Pursell 98-64.

But the intramural warfare went on. After the conference vote, the California delegation ousted Lewis from his seat on the Committee on Committees, replacing him with hard-core conservative Ron Packard. While Lewis was conservative enough for the conference, he was too moderate for many of his California colleagues.[33] Personality clashes also hurt him. William Dannemeyer bore an old grudge against Lewis, whom he blamed for his failure to win a seat on the Budget Committee.[34]

Two years later, Lewis faced yet another challenge, this time from Dick Armey of Texas, the bombthrowing conservative who had authored the 1990 no-tax-increase resolution. In this contest, Lewis had several problems. First, the loss of the Committee on Committees seat had robbed him of a source of influence. He tried to compensate by donating heavily to GOP candidates, but Armey also made substantial contributions. Though Armey's total giving fell below Lewis's, Armey gave more effectively by donating $14,400 to twenty-two freshmen *after* the November election, thereby avoiding some "wasted" donations to losers. Lewis made no post-election contributions.[35]

Second, Bill Clinton's victory obviated Lewis's appeal to GOP presidential loyalists. With a Democrat in the White House, Republicans no longer needed leaders who could work with the majority to pass the president's programs.

Third and most important, the 1992 election brought in forty-seven new Republicans, who made up more than a quarter of the total Conference membership. Although the secret ballot made it hard to determine how the new members voted, they appeared to be more conservative and confrontational than the members they replaced, so Armey probably gained from their arrival. Freshman Martin Hoke of Ohio said that between thirty to thirty-five of his classmates had voted for Armey.[36]

Armey won, albeit by only four votes. In contested races for secretary and vice chair, younger conservative bombthrowers from the South and West handily defeated older moderate responsible partners from the Northeast and Midwest. As mentioned above, the leadership team was now completely conservative and predominantly southern and western. Of the eight elected leaders, only Michel (born 1923) and Hyde (born 1924) belonged to the World War II generation: the next oldest leader was Armey, born in 1940.

And apart from Michel, all the leaders believed in partisan confrontation. The bent of the new team upset a number of responsible partners. Shortly after the election, Steve Gunderson quit as chief deputy whip for strategy. As he explained:

> [W]hen we looked at the leadership elections . . . where it became clear that every candidate who was the most conservative, who had the most strident tones in their campaign and in their congressional history was elected, many of us looked at the results of that and said this is not representative, not only of the Republican mainstream in the country, it's not representative of Republicans in the House of Representatives.[37]

For similar reasons, Fred Upton of Michigan left the post of deputy whip. Willis Gradison of Ohio, who had lost the Conference secretary race to DeLay, resigned from the House altogether, citing a lucrative job offer from a health-care interest group.

Change and Consequences

The changing face of the House GOP in the 1980s and 1990s was a mirror image of the Democrats in the 1970s. During that decade, a new crop of northern liberals increasingly dominated the Democratic Caucus.[38] Though frustrated with Carl Albert, they nonetheless sought to strengthen the Speakership because they hoped that the *next* Speaker would be more to their liking. This historical parallel helps explain why conservative bombthrowers wanted to centralize power within the Republican Party. By the late 1980s, they could tell that time was working against the factions that had once dominated the Conference. Strengthening the Republican Leader thus seemed a wise investment, for it seemed certain that one of their own would hold the job someday.

Early in the fall of 1993, Michel started hinting that he would retire. Gerald Solomon (R-New York) suggested himself as a logical successor: "He [Michel] often turns to me on various issues, because he knows I'm dependable and able to articulate positions of those of us who are Old Right."[39] Gingrich, however, was already rounding up his own votes. Three days after Michel officially announced his retirement, Gingrich held a press conference where he declared that he already had commitments of support from 106 colleagues, including forty of the freshmen.[40] Although Solomon initially voiced skepticism about this claim, he withdrew from the race a week later. It appeared that the succession was now complete.

Leadership Behavior

A close examination of Robert Michel and Newt Gingrich reveals a great deal about the House GOP's current composition and future direction. Like the great majority of House Republicans, both stand firmly on the right. A comparison of their vote ratings (Table 3-3) explodes the common misperception of an ideological gulf between them. Yet the similarity in their voting records masks significant differences in their governing philosophies.

Michel and Gingrich

At a press conference soon after his retirement announcement, Michel reflected on his arrival in Congress. His "junior chamber of commerce" supporters expected him simply to concentrate on cutting

Table 3-3
Michel and Gingrich Voting Scores in 1992

	Michel	Gingrich
Party Unity	87	94
Conservative Coalition	95	98
Presidential Support	93	88
ADA	10	10
AFL-CIO	25	22
Chamber of Commerce	88	88
Am. Conservative Union	87	100

Party unity, conservative coalition, and presidential support scores are normalized to eliminate the effects of absences. Sources: *Almanac of American Politics 1994* and *Politics in America: The 103d Congress.*

government: "And you know, that was about my charge. It wasn't anything about revolutionizing this or changing this or that, to that degree, other than on pretty much plain old philosophical ground." Looking ahead, he cautioned his colleagues: "I think I can encourage enough of the key people in our caucus to keep the big prize in mind: that we're a body politic here, a minority body, but we also have an obligation to the American people to be participants in the process, responsible participants in the process."[41]

Gingrich has also reflected on the responsibilities of legislative leaders, but with a different emphasis. Soon after his selection as whip in 1989, he wrote:

> Of course, one of my major goals will be to replace the Democrats as the majority party. That raises the obvious question—the most frequent one I am asked—whether I can at the same time work legislatively with House Democrats. The unequivocal answer is yes, if they are willing to engage in fair, honest bipartisanship.

Gingrich then described how he had worked with the majority on the House Administration Committee. But he added that "the area of ethics and corruption" constituted an exception—and his definition of corruption cast a wide net:

> I am even more confident that the American people are beginning to commit themselves to a generation of reform to overhaul the political corruption which has become endemic to the liberal welfare state. . . . So I will cooperate with the opposing party when we can get honest, fair, bipartisanship. But I will fight when the Democrats try to cheat and use the rules and other devices to avoid giving Republicans a fair break.[42]

These statements reveal contrasting visions of politics. A Burkean conservative, Michel distrusts abstractions, preferring balance and incremental change. Gingrich, on the other hand, sounds more like Thomas Paine, calling for blunt action against a clear evil: the "corrupt liberal welfare state." Both Michel and Gingrich, however, are accountable to the rank and file, who sometimes tug each man from his preferred style. The two leaders have thus had to take a step in each other's direction: Michel the conciliator has had to fight, while Gingrich the fighter has had to compromise.

Michel as Fighter

In the 102d Congress, Michel won a rules waiver that allowed Willis Gradison to become ranking Republican on Budget even though he had already served on the committee for the maximum six years. The bombthrowers disliked Michel's decision. Said one: "On the one hand, we're very loudly and very visibly opposing them [Democrats]. And then on the other hand, we're saying: 'Take me. I'm yours.' "[43]

At the same time, Michel acknowledged the bombthrowers when he transferred the ranking Republican slot on the Rules Committee from James Quillen (R-Tennessee) to Solomon. Quillen, though he had enjoyed working with House Democrats, wanted to avoid an intramural battle, so he gracefully stepped aside. The bombthrowers favored Solomon for his aggressiveness in fighting Democrats both in committee and on the floor. In an later interview, Michel said that he was happy with the Solomon choice:

> I just wanted to have someone—even though we were outnumbered two to one plus one with very little prospect of ever winning—at least someone vigorous enough, articulate enough, firebrand enough to make the case: "this is why this is wrong." And we know we're going to lose on the votes in the committee, but at least have the case made so there's some fodder there for the media to pick up and say, "Well, you know, maybe, you may have a point."

At times, Michel showed a tough partisan side that surprised the Democrats. In 1986, when the House was considering aid to the Nicaraguan rebels, the majority crafted a complex procedure that precluded a direct vote on President Reagan's proposal. At a closed-door conference, Michel asked Republicans to side with liberal Democrats to pass an amendment to bar military aid. The approval of that measure would block the more moderate amendment that the Democratic leadership really wanted. The maneuver worked, and the majority then halted further action on the bill. Paradoxically, the approval of the liberal amendment helped keep military aid alive. On the floor, Michel explained the maneuver to the shocked Democrats:

> When you have a rotten rule to play by, we are forced to be somewhat unconventional in our approach to the process. Our vote was the only way we had of telling the majority of the American public that we will not be a party to a procedure that debases the legislative process and demeans the ideals of comity and civility that lie at the heart of that process.[44]

Gingrich as Conciliator

As a backbencher, Gingrich had long attacked congressional pay increases; but after becoming whip, he supported a 1989 bill that combined a pay raise with ethics reform. In an unprecedented move, he joined with other Republican and Democratic leaders in signing a pledge not to use the pay vote as a campaign issue in the 1990 elections. The ethics reform affected his decision, but he probably also knew that many of his Republican colleagues simply wanted a higher salary.

Gingrich again surprised Washington during the 1990 budget talks, when he reportedly told Democratic negotiators: "I'm prepared to sponsor and support raising taxes" as part of a plan that also made massive spending cuts.[45] He later explained: "There got to be a point during the budget summit that I was beginning to listen carefully to liberal Democratic arguments and tried to figure out how I could agree with them. When I got home I realized, in fact, that was not why I got hired. I suddenly realized how real the 'Stockholm Syndrome' is—when you are captured by a terrorist and start identifying with the kidnapers."[46] Gingrich also bowed to the "responsible partners": "It is inherent in an honorable negotiator walking into a room, that if you get a good negotiation, that you have an obligation to co-sponsor it."[47] In the end, however, the product of the budget summit displeased many Republicans, and Gingrich led the fight against it.

After the divisive budget debacle, Gingrich reaffirmed his support for President Bush and called for greater party unity. At the 1991 Conservative Political Action Conference, Gingrich called it "a huge disservice to America when conservatives spend 60 percent to 80 percent of their time fighting over the level of perfection in their party." Tom DeLay replied: "That's not our line. We're having a struggle right now within the Republican Party. Basically, it's those who think they're here to govern and those who think they're here to take over a majority. I am not among those here to govern. I am here to take over a majority from the Democrats."[48] Vin Weber reflected on such disagreements: "There is no question that it creates a tension between Newt and folks in the conservative movement. Conservatives want aggressive leadership, and when you are in the leadership, it moderates your style and to some extent your substance."[49]

Leadership and the Future

As these examples suggest, institutional context not only influences which members ascend to the leadership (what Peters calls "natural selection"[50]), it also modifies their behavior once they get there.

Nevertheless, leaders are more than products of their setting. Individuals make a difference.

Observing the House Republicans in their permanent minority status raises three intriguing possibilities. First, the mix of members' goals changes over time. Second, institutional status (especially "permanent minority" status) affects personal goals. Third, party leaders can affect what the members want and how they see themselves. Scholars who focus on the majority party may underestimate the conflict between reelection and power within the chamber. House Republicans, however, are torn between their individual interest in reelection and their long-term party interest in regaining a majority.

As a leader, Gingrich goes beyond merely servicing members' desires as he finds them. Preaching about "the necessary revolution," he tries to change what members want. In persuading his colleagues to elect him as whip and support him for Leader, Gingrich has gotten them to think about a new philosophy for a new day. It is difficult to conclude that House Republicans follow him out of a narrow concern for reelection.

Gingrich warns his colleagues against becoming creatures of an institution that is rigged against them. The 1980s witnessed a sharp rise in partisan voting in the House, stemming in part from the increasing homogeneity of House Democratic and Republican electorates, but also from the majority's increased use of restrictive rules to structure debate.[51] Through these procedures, House Democrats could thwart the efforts of House Republicans to nationalize issues through high-profile floor votes. House Republicans were convinced that such votes would resonate with voters and hurt Democratic incumbents. To the GOP's frustration, House Democrats largely succeeded in narrowing the scope of conflict and avoiding electoral accountability.

Gingrich and other leaders try to escape this trap by influencing the larger public agenda. They operate on the assumption that they *can* change voters' preferences, and that they have to go beyond the House walls to do so. Coordinated town meetings, media events, televised speeches—all are efforts to redefine legislative leadership as reaching past the floor to the entire country.

There is a distinct irony to such efforts. If they succeed, and the House GOP does win a majority, the leaders who devised them might not be secure in their positions. Once in the majority, the party might apply new criteria in picking leaders. The speaker's job differs greatly from that of minority Leader. In choosing the latter, members must decide who can best cope with the constraints of minority status. In choosing the former, they must decide who can do the best job of running the institution, meting out real power, and crafting legislation that will become law. In other words, the choice would no longer be between confrontation and accommodation (aside from relations with the White House), but among different prospects of substantive performance. The Democrats have tended to choose their leaders from their whip system, and for good reason: whip duties allow members to prove their political intelligence and ability to manage detail.[52] In the majority, Republicans may follow the same pattern. That is perhaps why Gingrich started with the whip's job rather than another leadership position.

A similar calculation may explain his intense efforts to help President Clinton win House approval of the North American Free Trade Agreement in 1993. Gingrich showed that, where necessary, he could work with a president of the opposite party and actually pass legislation rather than just score partisan points. If the GOP ever does win a majority, Gingrich can point to the NAFTA victory as evidence of his qualification to be speaker.

As of the early 1990s, any serious thoughts of a GOP speakership remained premature. The House Republicans still faced many obstacles, not the least of which was the power of the House Democrats.

Notes

1. Edmund Burke, *Reflections on the Revolution in France* (Garden City, N.Y.: Doubleday/Anchor Books, 1973), 53.

2. For good summaries of the "contextualist" view, see Frank H. Mackaman, ed., *Understanding Congressional Leadership* (Washington, D.C.: CQ Press, 1981).

3. Richard B. Cheney and Lynne V. Cheney, *Kings of the Hill: Power and Personality in the House of Representatives* (New York: Continuum, 1983), 197.

4. Irwin B. Arieff, "House Democrats, GOP Elect Leaders, Draw Battle Lines," *Congressional Quarterly Weekly Report*, December 13, 1980, 3549.

5. Don Wolfensberger, "The Role of Party Caucuses in the House of Representatives" (paper presented at the annual conference of the American Political Science Association, Washington, D.C., September 1–4, 1988).

6. "Dick Armey Prepares a GOP Counterattack," *Human Events*, January 30, 1993, 3.

7. Dick Armey, "Your Future Health Plan," *Wall Street Journal*, October 13, 1993, A16; *The Limbaugh Letter*, November 1993, 11.

8. House Republican Policy Committee, "Republican Policy Statement on the Crime Caper of 1993," November 4, 1993.

9. William F. Connelly, Jr., "The House Republican Policy Committee: Then and Now" (paper presented at the annual conference of the American Political Science Association, Washington, D.C., September 1–4, 1988).

10. Jason W. Klawitter, "The Role of the Republican Research Committee: A Look at Policy Shapers of Republican Leadership," unpublished manuscript, Claremont McKenna College, Claremont, California, 1989.

11. Charles Cook, "Can a Reinvigorated NRCC Fulfill House Expectations in '94?" *Roll Call*, December 2, 1993, 8.

12. Robin Kolodny, "More Leaders Leading Less? The Proliferation of Party Leadership Positions in Congress" (paper presented at the annual conference of the American Political Science Association, Washington, D.C., September 2–5, 1993).

13. Charles O. Jones, *Party and Policymaking: The House Republican Policy Committee* (New Brunswick, N.J.: Rutgers University Press, 1964), 22.

14. Charles O. Jones, *The Minority Party in Congress* (Boston: Little, Brown, 1970), 38.

15. Robert L. Peabody, "Political Parties: House Republican Leadership," in *American Political Institutions and Public Policy: Five Contemporary Studies*, ed. Allan P. Sindler (Boston: Little, Brown, 1969), 198–99.

16. Randall B. Ripley, *Party Leaders in the House of Representatives* (Washington, D.C.: Brookings, 1967), 190.

17. Craig Winneker, "Heard on the Hill," *Roll Call*, December 2, 1991, 19.

18. Quoted in Nicol C. Rae, *The Decline and Fall of the Liberal Republicans From 1952 to the Present* (New York: Oxford University Press, 1989), 185.

19. Quoted in Fred Barnes, "Split in the Ranks," *The New Republic*, May 18, 1985, 11.

20. Quoted in Margaret Shapiro, "House GOP Revolt Was Fed by Years of Feeling Ignored," *Washington Post*, December 15, 1985, A6.

21. Quoted in David E. Rosenbaum, "Years of Republican Frustration Underlay House Revolt on Taxes," *New York Times*, December 15, 1985, 38.

22. Quoted in Stephen E. Nordlinger, "House GOP Revolt Bares Split Long in Making," *Baltimore Sun*, December 15, 1985, 14A.

23. Quoted in Shapiro, "House GOP Revolt," A1.

24. Quoted in Edward Walsh, "GOP Points Fingers on Tax-Bill Blunders," *Washington Post*, December 19, 1985, A6.

25. Quoted in Robert Timberg and Stephen E. Nordlinger, "Kemp Played Crucial Role in Saving Bill," *Baltimore Sun*, December 18, 1985, 1A.

26. House Republican Conference, resolutions adopted December 9, 1986.

27. Quoted in Mike Mills, "GOP Selects Leaders: Michel, Cheney, Lewis," *Congressional Quarterly Weekly Report*, December 10, 1988, 3475.

28. "The New House Leaders: Bipartisan Compromisers," *National Journal*, December 13, 1980, 2136.

29. Michael Barone and Grant Ujifusa, *The Almanac of American Politics 1990* (Washington, D.C.: National Journal Press, 1989), 38.

30. Quoted in Bill McKenzie, "A Conversation with Newt Gingrich," *Ripon Forum*, May 1989, 3.

31. Ralph Z. Hallow, "Hyde Eyes Run for GOP Whip; Battle of Conservatives Looms," *Washington Times*, March 15, 1989, A3.

32. Quoted in Jim Drinkard, "House Republicans Re-Elect Leadership," Associated Press, December 3, 1990.

33. Larry Liebert, "Splintering Among State's Republicans in Congress," *San Francisco Chronicle*, December 27, 1990, A23.

34. Janet Hook, "Grudges on the Hill: The Hidden Motive," *Congressional Quarterly Weekly Report*, August 31, 1991, 2398.

35. Tim Curran, "Rivals Armey and Lewis Give GOP Candidates $160,000 Before Faceoff," *Roll Call*, December 21, 1992, 2.

36. Clifford Krauss, "Staunch Conservative Wins GOP Post in House," *New York Times*, December 8, 1992, A12.

37. *Fox Morning News* interview, Reuter transcript, January 6, 1993.

38. Barbara Sinclair, *Majority Leadership in the U.S. House* (Baltimore: Johns Hopkins University Press, 1983), 7.

39. Quoted in Timothy J. Burger, "With Michel Exit Likely, Gingrich, Hyde, Solomon Start Race for Minority Leader," *Roll Call*, September 13, 1993, 17.

40. Clifford Krauss, "Gingrich Stakes Claim To Minority Leadership," *New York Times*, October 8, 1993, A17.

41. News conference with Robert Michel, Reuter transcript, October 4, 1993.

42. Newt Gingrich, "The Gingrich Manifesto," *Washington Post*, April 9, 1989, B2.

43. Quoted in Major Garrett, "Michel Deals for Moderate," *Washington Times*, January 3, 1991, A6.

44. *Congressional Record*, daily ed., April 16, 1986, H1891.

45. Quoted in John E. Yang, "Rep. Gingrich 'Prepared' to Back Increase in Taxes," *Washington Post*, July 20, 1990, A6.

46. Quoted in Richard L. Berke, "As Guerrilla or General, Gingrich has a Mission," *New York Times*, July 19, 1990, A18.

47. Quoted in Susan F. Rasky, "GOP Whip Reverses Tax Stance," *New York Times*, July 20, 1990, A10.

48. Quoted in Ralph Z. Hallow, "Gingrich Challenged by GOP Brethren," *Washington Times*, February 8, 1991, A4.

49. Quoted in James A. Barnes, "Still Missing Reagan," *National Journal*, March 2, 1991, 513.

50. Ronald M. Peters, Jr., *The American Speakership: The Office in Historical Perspective* (Baltimore: Johns Hopkins University Press, 1991), 141.

51. Michael J. Malbin, "Political Parties Across the Separation of Powers,"

in *American Political Parties and Constitutional Politics*, ed. Peter W. Schramm and Bradford P. Wilson (Lanham, Md.: Rowman and Littlefield, 1993), 82–85.

52. David T. Canon, "The Institutionalization of Leadership in the U.S. Congress," *Legislative Studies Quarterly* 14 (August 1989): 421.

Chapter 4

The War on the Floor

In 1986, political scientist Norman Ornstein asked: "What happens after a majority has been in for a long time? The majority begins to believe that it is their God-given right to be in the majority and the minority begins to get more and more obstreperous and obdurate."[1] On each side, candid lawmakers saw some truth in Ornstein's assessment. Rules Committee Chairman Joe Moakley (D-Massachusetts) acknowledged the House Democrats' typical attitude toward the GOP: "Hey, we've got the votes. Let's vote. Screw you."[2] And Jerry Lewis (R-California) said of the Republicans: "As far as influencing what happens inside the House, we have just enough votes to be irresponsible."[3]

Both Moakley and Lewis voiced optimism that relations between the parties would improve after Speaker Jim Wright's painful downfall. Their hopes proved forlorn. Under Speaker Thomas Foley, the majority further curbed the minority party's role in floor activity.[4] On the Republican side, confrontationists gained more strength, partially in reaction to the perceived abuses of the majority party.

The very character of minority status was changing. In the age of House czars such as Thomas Reed and Joseph Cannon, the minority party could bide its time and plan what it would do in the majority. Between the Progressive Era and the 1970s, the minority could frequently take a real part in legislating. By the Foley speakership, the minority party was usually reduced to the status of commentator: when it really counted, House Republicans could seldom make laws.

The resulting frustration reached across the GOP's "Great Divide." Many of those who preached accommodation started to think that the majority would not give them a fair hearing. The supporters of confrontation and national political strategies were blocked from waging their kind of battle in regular floor debate. Increasingly, House Republicans could gain attention only through the exercise or threat of disruptive tactics.

The "War on the Floor" illustrates the reciprocal influence of politicians and institutions. The members' beliefs shape the House's procedures, which influence legislative outcomes, which in turn color the members' beliefs. House Democrats see recent congressional history as a series of fights to protect the institution against Republican irresponsibility. House Republicans see it as a series of fights to stop an increasingly arrogant majority from trampling their rights.

Roots of Rancor

The House's partisan conflict is the offspring of two ironies. First, the practices that Republicans denounce as "undemocratic" stem in part from procedural reforms that were supposed to make the House more open and accountable. Second, although Republicans accuse the Democratic leaders of a power-driven devotion to the status quo, those leaders came to office as policy-oriented agents of change.

During the first fifteen or so years of what would become "permanent minority" status, Republicans had little inkling of the troubles ahead. Despite Democratic majorities in both chambers, the minority could often win legislative victories by making common cause with conservative southern Democrats. After the GOP's 1966 midterm comeback, wrote Charles O. Jones, it sometimes "appeared that the Republicans were the majority and the Democrats the minority."[5]

The Democratic Caucus, however, was undergoing changes that would eventually undercut GOP power. Since the 1950s, the House Democrats had comprised a growing faction of "programmatic liberals," younger members who cared more about policy ideas than political patronage. Over time, they made up a larger and larger bloc within the Caucus, especially after 1974. Meanwhile, the enfranchisement of black voters helped draw white Southern lawmakers into the Democratic ideological mainstream.[6] As the party's center of gravity shifted leftward, the programmatic liberals seized the opportunity to reform House procedure. They were not only interested in individual power: if that were the case, they could merely have waited their turn in the seniority system. Rather, they wanted to restructure the institution so they could launch policy initiatives that the old congressional regime would have scuttled.[7]

Liberal Democrats paid close attention to committees, where conservative Republicans had often won quiet victories. "To a junior Republican, there was something to look forward to, even if he wasn't going to be in the majority," said a senior GOP lawmaker. "[Being ranking member] wasn't the same as being chairman, but it was the next best thing."[8] With the help of some liberal Republicans, they passed legislation encouraging committees to hold their formal meetings in the open.[9] "In closed meetings, Republican members used to be able to cut a deal and drive the chairman," a veteran staffer told us. Now that committee Democrats worked under the wary eye of their party caucus, they balked at striking controversial bargains with the minority. Republicans suffered a further disadvantage when shadows appeared in the new daylight: Democrats on some committees started to make decisions at caucuses that were closed to the minority.

In 1975, House Democrats undid an earlier reform when they restored proxy voting in committees—a practice that weakened the Republicans' leverage by keeping them from taking advantage of Democratic absences.[10] Of the twenty-eight standing and select committees in the 102nd Congress (1991–93), twenty-three permitted proxy voting and nineteen allowed one-third of the membership to constitute a quorum to conduct business, except for reporting measures.[11]

The shift of power to subcommittees also hurt the GOP. Subcommittee chairs were often more liberal—and less likely to work with Republicans—than the committee chairs. Party ratios on subcommittees tilted even more heavily toward the majority than full committee ratios.[12]

On Public Works and some other committees, an ethic of bipartisanship still allowed the Republicans a smidgen of influence, especially with distributive issues such as pork-barrel projects. When committees handled broad national issues with ideological overtones, Republicans often found themselves on the outside. In 1986, Budget Committee member Lynn Martin (R-Illinois) complained: "We received this document [a list of committee amendments] at 8:45 last night. We hope that if we are ever in the majority we will remember to treat the minority as it should be treated." Charles Schumer (D-New York) answered: "It's our ball. They can play or they can go home."[13]

Meanwhile, Republicans were shifting their partisan energy to the House chamber. Though televising of floor debate did not by itself generate more floor amendments, it did give frustrated Republicans a way to take their case to the C-SPAN audience, both through one-minute addresses at the start of the day and one-hour "special orders" at the end.[14] New voting rules also drew Republicans to the floor. Until the 1970s, the *Congressional Record* had not published individual members' votes on floor amendments.[15] Liberal Democrats led the push for recorded votes, thinking that greater accountability would benefit their side. By the late 1970s, however, Republicans were using recorded votes to bog down Democratic bills and force the majority to cast embarrassing votes on controversial issues.

At this point, centralized leadership came to the Democrats' rescue. A few years earlier, they had strengthened the speakership by giving it more say in bill referrals and committee assignments. By empowering the speaker to nominate the chair and majority members of the Rules Committee, they endowed the office with great influence over floor procedure. This influence proved a powerful weapon in the hands of a tough partisan—Tip O'Neill (D-Massachusetts). GOP Leader John Rhodes (R-Arizona) had called O'Neill "the most partisan man I have ever known" and recounted an O'Neill warning: "Republicans are just going to have to get it through their heads that they are not going to write legislation!"[16]

O'Neill did not have to give detailed daily orders to the Rules Committee, because his intense partisanship usually gave a clear sign of what he wanted. Under the new speaker, remembered a House Republican leadership aide, "The degree of gamesmanship jumped exponentially." The Rules Committee responded to GOP floor tactics with restrictive special rules that let the majority set the terms of debate, including which amendments could be offered and in what order.

As Table 4-1 indicates, O'Neill started a trend that turned restrictive rules from an occasional expedient in the 1970s to a standard practice in the early 1990s. Although restrictive rules are sometimes useful as a way to prevent endless delays, they have become less defensible as they have become more common. In the words of Mann and Ornstein: "Taken together, however, they constitute a disregard for minority rights, the rights of individual members, and a dismissal of the constructive role the minority or other dissenters can play in offering alternatives and pointing out flaws in a pending measure."[17]

This procedural warfare has had a number of extensions and refinements. Some examples:

- *Limitation Amendments.* When appropriations bills were on the floor, Republicans had often offered limitation amendments, forbidding the use of public money for specified purposes. In 1983, the

Table 4-1
Restrictive Rules, 95th-103d Congresses

Congress (years)	Total rules	% Restrictive
95th (1977–78)	211	15
96th (1979–80)	214	25
97th (1981–82)	120	25
98th (1983–84)	155	32
99th (1985–86)	115	43
100th (1987–88)	123	46
101st (1989–90)	104	55
102nd (1991–92)	109	66
103d (1993)*	41	77

*The figure for 1993 is through November 20.
Total rules include all order of business resolutions reported from the Rules Committee that provide for the initial consideration of legislation, except rules on appropriations bills that only waive points of order. Restrictive rules are those that limit the number of amendments that can be offered, and include "modified open" and "modified closed" rules as well as completely closed rules, and rules providing for consideration in the House instead of the Committee of the Whole. The percentages are restrictive rules as a percent of total rules granted. (Source: Material entered by Representative Gerald Solomon, *Congressional Record*, daily ed., November 22, 1993, H10723.)

majority enacted a rules change making it much more difficult to obtain a floor vote on such amendments. The change worked, and the number of limitation amendments plummeted.[18]

- *Motion to Recommit*. Opponents of a bill can enjoy one last chance to get a recorded vote on their own proposals by moving to return the bill to committee, with instructions to amend it. The recommittal motion has customarily been the minority party's prerogative. In the 95th Congress, the Rules Committee issued three floor rules that limited the minority's right to offer such motions. In the 100th Congress this practice reached a peak with twenty-four restrictive rules, and the number dropped to twenty-one in the following Congress. Mainly because of GOP complaints against such rules, in the 102d Congress the number had shrunk to seven.[19]

- *Budget Act Waivers*. Republicans have sometimes tried to fight legislation by raising points of order under provisions of the Budget Act of 1974. In response, the Rules Committee has offered floor rules waiving such points of order. (Some waivers apply to certain Budget Act provisions, while others set aside all standing House rules.) In the 96th Congress, 19 percent of all rules contained one or more such waivers. This figure peaked in the 99th Congress at 65 percent. Then followed a slight decline to 51 percent in the 100th, 56 percent in the 101st, and 47 percent in the 102d.[20]

- *Suspension of the Rules.* Under this procedure, bills are debatable for forty minutes, are not subject to amendment, and must pass by a two-thirds vote. In the past, the House typically employed suspensions mainly for minor and noncontroversial bills; but since the O'Neill speakership the majority has also used the procedure for important and contentious issues. In 1983, O'Neill even tried to use it for the Equal Rights Amendment, but the maneuver failed when some ERA supporters objected to changing the U.S. Constitution under such a procedure. The number of measures that have passed under suspension rose from 38 percent of all bills passed in the 95th Congress to 52 percent in the 102d Congress.[21] As a partisan political maneuver, suspensions depend upon GOP disunity, because if Republicans hold more than one-third of the seats, no suspension motion can pass if Republicans unite against it.

House Democrats cite principled reasons for curbing minority influence. Sam Gejdenson (D-Connecticut), a confrontational member of the majority, put it this way:

[I] get the sense that Republican Members of Congress would like to legislate themselves into majority status, that their inability to win a majority of the House is—what they would like to do is kind of get a legislative process that gives them veto over getting the bills through the process. As the majority, our job at the end of the day is getting the bill through and onto the President's desk. And, just as in the Senate, the filibuster gives the minority the ability to, one, represent the minority, it sometimes gives the minority the ability to thwart the will of the majority. That is the balance I think we have to seek in both institutions and the danger is if we pay too much attention to every desire of the minority in this institution we will never get anything done.[22]

Many House Democrats have also noted that the GOP has sometimes benefited from restrictive rules, and that the Republicans controlled the White House for twelve years under Reagan and Bush. In the middle of the second Reagan administration, Majority Leader

Thomas Foley (D-Washington) said: "There are two minorities in the House of Representatives—the Democratic minority vis-à-vis the administration, and a Republican minority vis-à-vis the House."[23]

Previous spans of divided government—the Eisenhower years of 1955–61 and the Nixon-Ford years of 1969–77—stirred less interparty turmoil than did the 1980s. Eisenhower and congressional Democrats worked closely together. Nixon mounted less a partisan challenge to congressional Democrats than an institutional challenge to Congress. The 1980 elections restored divided government—with a difference. Unlike Nixon, Reagan entered with a conservative agenda, a Senate majority, and a feisty House GOP conference. Sensing an unprecedented threat to social programs, House Democrats thought they had to fight back; and to do so, they first had to overcome the House Republicans. What the majority saw as a lonely battle with a mighty White House, the minority saw as a massive assault on their already-humble status.

House politics was bound to get mean. John LeBoutillier (R-New York), a member of the class of 1980, said that O'Neill was "big, fat and out of control just like the federal government" and that he "personifies everything about politics that the public hates today."[24] Political scientists and other commentators have documented similar breaches of comity on the part of congressional Republicans.[25] What has received less attention is that House Democrats also raised the ante of personal abuse. Two examples:

• In 1984, Tony Coelho (D-California), chair of the Democratic Congressional Campaign Committee, circulated among House Democrats a magazine article making ugly assertions about Newt Gingrich's private life. In 1987, when Gingrich was calling for an ethics investigation of Speaker Wright, Mervyn Dymally (D-California) inserted long excerpts from this article into the *Congressional Record*.[26]

• Speaker O'Neill said of President Reagan: "The evil is in the White House at the present time. And that evil is a man who has no care and no concern for the working class of America and the future generations of America, and who likes to ride a horse. He's cold. He's mean. He's got ice water for blood."[27]

Scenes from the Partisan Conflict on Capitol Hill

The House's partisan conflict has played out in a series of tumultuous episodes, which illustrate how the politics of procedural wrangling and personal abuse has affected the institution. These incidents have had a cumulative impact: politicians have long memories, so each new skirmish has become part of the background for subsequent fights.

The 1981 Budget

In 1981, Speaker O'Neill had promised that President Reagan would get a House vote on the spending cuts that he had proposed. The House Rules Committee did provide for floor action on such cuts as part of budget reconciliation legislation. But instead of allowing for the single vote the Republicans had wanted, the proposed rule would have had members vote on six separate pieces, stripped of GOP provisions to sweeten the package by easing some of the cuts. To support the package, lawmakers would have had to cast six public votes against some popular programs, including child nutrition, student loans, and federal pensions.

Referring to the Democratic decision to remove the "sweeteners," Republican Leader Michel said: "These are no longer our amendments that are made in order. They are bastards of the worst order for which we disclaim parental responsibility. . . . It is a rotten rule. It is what you would expect to cram down the throats of a party of nincompoops."[28] With some conservative Democrats, Republicans won enough votes to defeat this rule and substitute one that provided for a vote on a complete GOP package. In this case, the Democrats argued in subsequent sessions, the Republicans had used a tactic that they later deplored: forcing a single vote on omnibus legislation.

After the vote on the rule, the Republican Leader's office sent the reconciliation measure to the printer. The next day, it came back with jumbled pages and scribbles in the margins. In debate, Democrats mocked the sloppy document. Meanwhile, a top GOP leadership staffer made a discovery:

> I picked up the rumor that the bill hadn't gotten to the printer on time. I knew I had gotten it to the clerk by 5 PM. I checked and found that the Government Printing Office hadn't gotten it until several hours later. I learned that [Vic] Fazio [D-California] had a messenger bring it back to him in a room in the Capitol. [Phil] Burton [D-California] had put Fazio up to it. The Democrats wanted to get an advance look at it, but when they tried to put it back together, they didn't know the right order.

The aide told Michel, who then repeated the story on the floor. Burton replied that he and Fazio were "only ascertaining as to its bulk whether or not it lent itself to reproduction."[29] Burton said that after they saw that it was too thick to copy quickly, they returned it to the messenger. According to the aide, however, Michel's public charge had changed the chamber's atmosphere: no longer were the Republicans on the defensive.

The GOP won the reconciliation vote, a victory that left the Democrats vengeful. And the majority's maneuvers had left the Republicans suspicious.

Camscam

In the spring of 1984, Republican aide Frank Gregorsky wrote a report accusing congressional Democrats of a "radical worldview" in which "there is no crime by a Communist army or government that can't either be trivialized or blamed on America."[30] On May 8, Newt Gingrich and Robert Walker (R-Pennsylvania) presented the report in speeches aimed mainly at the C-SPAN audience. This report enraged Democrats. Said David Obey (D-Wisconsin): "[T]oday's modern descendants of Joe McCarthy may be a little bit prettier and a little more skilled in the use of television; they are certainly no less comfortable in the use of innuendo than was the late Senator from my own State."[31]

The report criticized O'Neill's friend, Rep. Edward Boland (D-Massachusetts), and O'Neill wanted retribution. Control of the House cameras gave him a weapon. Until this time, the cameras had only shown the lawmaker who was speaking at any moment, so television viewers could not see how many others were present. In his memoirs, O'Neill described his counterattack: "The next day, when Robert Walker of Pennsylvania tried something similar, I called Charlie Rose, the member in charge of television in the House, and told him I thought the cameras should pan the entire chamber. Charlie informed the camera crew, and when they showed the empty hall, Walker looked like a fool."[32]

In the middle of his speech, in which he was charging that Democrats had falsified congressional documents, Walker noted O'Neill's action: "It is one more example of how this body is run; the kind of arrogance of power that the members are given that kind of change with absolutely no warning." He also spotted the head of the Democratic Congressional Campaign Committee: "Mr. Coelho has talked in recent weeks about shutting off these special orders and not allowing them to even be seen in the countryside. And he stands in the back of the chamber now smiling."[33] Other Republicans contended that O'Neill had abused his authority to pull a cheap trick, and that the issue was less about camera angles than artibrary behavior. Eight years later, O'Neill said: "I didn't give them notification, and I was wrong on that."[34]

The week after what Republicans called "Camscam," the confrontation took new dimensions. Democrats accused Gingrich and Walker of failing to give advance notice to the colleagues they criticized. In an unusual move, O'Neill went down into the well to join the debate. He said:

> There is no question in my mind that the arguments and statements that I said on this floor came to me by complaint of the Members. First, that they had not been notified. I do not believe that they were notified. . . . My personal opinion is this: You deliberately stood in that well before an empty House and challenged these people, and you challenged their Americanism, and it is the lowest thing that I have ever seen in my 32 years in Congress.[35]

Republican whip Trent Lott (R-Mississippi) then moved that O'Neill's words be "taken down"; that is, ruled out of order. On the advice of the parliamentarian, the presiding member ruled favorably on the motion: "The Chair feels that that type of characterization should not be used in debate."[36] This ruling represented the first such reproach for a House speaker in nearly two centuries.

The confrontation reached the front pages and instantly made Gingrich a national figure. At a party conference, Republican members hailed Gingrich and reviled O'Neill. Confrontationist Vin Weber (R-Minnesota) called O'Neill "one of the cheapest, meanest politicians to occupy that office in this century." Michel reportedly responded: "I'll have to agree with you. To have this man act the way this one has is unheard of."[37]

The Democrats took their own shots. When asked if he planned to listen to further special orders by Gingrich, Walker, and Weber, the speaker replied: "What are the names of the Three Stooges? I think I'll let Larry, Moe, and Curly talk to themselves."[38] In a press release, Coelho referred to an anti-O'Neill GOP publicity effort as a "lie and buy" campaign.[39]

"Camscam" had a lasting impact. Democrats feared a resurgence of McCarthyism. On the GOP side, even some responsible partners began to soften their resistance to tougher tactics. Said Hamilton Fish (R-New York), a model of patrician reserve: "Those of us who were not inclined to confrontation have now discovered that pressure, and tough pressure, is the way to get results."[40]

Coelho argued that the affair would help Democrats win seats: "A 100-vote margin is not enough for us. We'd like to have 150."[41] Those words would soon echo ominously in Republican ears. They would charge the House Democrats with stealing a congressional seat.

McIntyre and McCloskey

After the 1984 elections, Indiana's Republican Secretary of State certified Republican Rick McIntyre as the winner over incumbent Democrat Frank McCloskey in the eighth congressional district. The race was extremely close, so on January 3, 1985, Majority Leader Jim Wright introduced a resolution to declare the seat vacant pending an investigation by the House Administration Committee. On a party-line vote, the House agreed.

The committee delegated the issue to a task force, which Republicans suspected of partisan bias. Fearing that the majority was arranging to rig the outcome, the GOP decided to strike first. During a *pro forma* session on March 4, Michel surprised the Democrats by offering a resolution to seat McIntyre provisionally. Democrats had not expected any serious business on the floor that day, so many were absent. The GOP whip organization tried to take advantage of these absences by getting most of the Republicans into the chamber. Former Representative Otis Pike (D-New York), then a columnist, picked up the story:

> One of the glories of being in the majority is that you not only control the schedule, you control the clock. Rep. Bill Alexander, a Democratic whip, moved that Michel's resolution be referred to the same committee that already had the issue. Then he stalled. . . . All the time Alexander was reading, planes, trains, and cars were bringing Democrats to Washington. When he finished, there were 40 minutes of time left for debate. Eighteen minutes later, there were still 30 minutes left for debate.[42]

O'Neill said: "I am shocked at the leadership on the Republican side." Michel responded that his side could not "wait for the majority in this House to find a way to seat someone other than one duly elected. . . ."[43] The Democrats got enough members into the chamber to pass Alexander's motion by a single vote.

On March 11, Bill Thomas (R-California) walked out of the task force, telling the Democratic members that they had "set up rules so your guy can win. I've tried to participate in this process, but by a 2-1 vote, I'm superfluous."[44] Thomas did attend subsequent meetings, where the issue came down to thirty-two absentee ballots. Republicans argued that the task force had accepted similar ballots, but rejected the thirty-two because Democrat McCloskey now had a slim lead. (A newspaper poll of the disputed absentee voters later revealed that their ballots would have elected the Republican.[45]) Democrats said that the thirty-two ballots differed in significant ways from those that had been counted. On April 18, the task force unofficially declared McCloskey the winner by four votes.

Five days later, the House Administration Committee adopted the task force report. The vote was 12-0, with the GOP members walking out. House Republicans were all angry with the Democrats, but they disagreed on how to respond. The bombthrowers wanted to bring the House to an indefinite halt. The responsible partners were willing to stage protests, but then they wanted to resume normal business. "It does not hurt to shoot a few warning shots across the bow," said Tom Tauke (R-Iowa). "On the other hand, the majority of Republicans know that shutting down the House is not a viable option."[46]

When the issue reached the full House, bile filled floor debate. Robert Walker damned "politicians who are willing to lie, cheat and steal. . . ." Byron Dorgan (D-North Dakota) said "that those who use the words 'cheat, lie, steal' do a great disservice to this House."[47] The House voted 236-190 to seat McCloskey, with all Republicans and ten Democrats voting no. When the result was announced, Republicans joined together to stage a symbolic walkout. This unity started to crack a few minutes later when Michel returned to the chamber to shake McCloskey's hand. The confrontationists murmured that the hand-shake was a sign of irresolution, while Michel firmly insisted that it was a gesture of goodwill.

The obstructionist ardor dwindled as cross-cutting pressures came into play. Even the fiercest partisans have to pay attention to their districts—and few constituents knew or cared about this dispute. Furthermore, conservative Republicans could not advance President Reagan's legislative program in a paralyzed House. "With Republicans controlling the White House the question is how can you be confrontational without holding things up?" said Gingrich. "The reality of it is the activists are going to be in the minority."[48]

Still, most Republicans remained bitter toward the House Democrats, especially campaign chief Tony Coelho. Said one:

I don't think this was Tip's doing. With Tip, it would have been like a Hitchcock movie: no fingerprints, no body. Here it was like a Brian dePalma movie: you saw the knife go in and the blood splatter all over. That's the way Coelho works.

In a later interview, this Republican would note that although the 1986 House elections produced three tight GOP victories, Democrats did not seek to overturn the results:

So you've got to go back to the McIntyre-McCloskey race and ask: Why that case and why then? This had nothing to do with McIntyre and McCloskey and everything to do with Tony Coelho trying to punish the Republicans for statements that some Republicans had been making about him.

According to House Democrats, however, their task force members refused even to discuss the issue with the campaign committee.[49] The Democrats also had a simple account of why they treated the McCloskey case differently: unlike the others, the McCloskey case involved their incumbent—and legislative parties take care of their own. Coelho blamed the GOP: "Which side began targeting opposition leadership members? Which began running negative and legally questionable media campaigns? Which ran ads with a lookalike actor depicting unfairly the speaker of the House?"[50]

The McIntyre-McCloskey fight increased GOP frustrations. At the height of the controversy, one Republican leader said: "At least half a dozen members have decided in the last 24 hours to leave."[51] Other members decided that they would rather fight than quit. Said Dick Cheney: "What choice does a self-respecting Republican have . . . except confrontation? If you play by the rules, the Democrats change the rules so they can win. There's absolutely nothing to be gained by cooperating with the Democrats at this point."[52]

Wright's Fights and the Long Count

Soon after the McIntyre-McCloskey fight, the conflict almost broke into real fisticuffs. Majority Leader Jim Wright (D-Texas), chairing the Committee of the Whole, seemed to miscount the members requesting a roll-call vote. When Dan Lungren (R-California) and Robert Walker (R-Pennsylvania) took exception, Wright told Lungren: "I am smiling because I am trying to hold inside how I feel. I want to come down off here and punch you and Mr. Walker in the mouth."[53] Wright later apologized.

In January 1987, Wright succeeded Tip O'Neill as speaker. Because of incidents such as the Lungren face-off, many Republicans thought that Wright would bring an even higher level of partisanship to the House. In public, however, some Republicans hoped for the best. Even Newt Gingrich recalled some gracious acts by Wright and said: "Things like that—if he does it—draw 90 percent of the poison out of this place."[54]

Years before, Wright had worked in the ideological center, but he turned left as O'Neill's retirement loomed. Otherwise, said a Democratic leader, "He couldn't be elected speaker. It's that simple."[55] A GOP leader disdained his shifts: "I don't think he's got the stature inside the Democratic Party or the House at large that would allow him to say, 'Hey that's crazy.' He knuckles under."

In the 100th Congress (1987–89), President Reagan was buckling under the triple burden of Iran-Contra, the Democratic takeover of the Senate, and his looming retirement.[56] After six years of divided government, House Democrats at last saw an opening for their policy agenda, and they expected their leadership to knock down any internal obstacles. Consequently, the trend toward restrictive rules continued.

On October 29, 1987, which Republicans would call "Black Thursday," this trend had dramatic consequences both for the House and for Wright himself. On that day, the House took up a budget reconciliation bill. Under Wright's direction, the Rules Committee had crafted a "self-executing" rule attaching ten Democratic amendments to the bill without separate votes. These amendments included a $6 billion welfare-reform package.[57] Republicans, as well as some Democrats, argued that such an important measure should require a separate vote. After Democratic opposition defeated the rule, Michel asked the speaker to set the bill aside pending talks with the president and Senate. "Michel made a very gracious and graceful statement," said a top Republican, "but the speaker basically said 'buzz off.'" Wright got the Rules Committee to report a new rule (minus the welfare provisions).

A two-thirds vote was required to return the bill to the floor on the same day. To bypass this requirement, Wright had the House adjourn and immediately reconvene for a new "legislative day"—a maneuver that required a mere majority and on which Democrats felt bound to follow the Speaker. This tactic stunned the GOP. A conservative

Republican from California had this sarcastic exchange with the new majority leader, Thomas Foley (D-Washington):

Mr. Dannemeyer: Mr. Speaker, Genesis tells us our Lord created the world in seven days. We are now witnessing the creation of an eighth day. I just ask the gentleman: Does he have a name for this new creation?
Mr. Foley: Yes: it is called the Guaranteed Deficit Reduction Reconciliation Act.[58]

Surprise turned to fury after the final roll call. The bill stood one vote short when Wright announced that all voting time had expired. Republicans shouted at him to make the result official. Then—even though the clock had run out—his aide John Mack brought Jim Chapman (D-Texas) back to the well to switch from nay to aye. The bill passed by one vote.

Republicans booed the result and assailed the Democratic leadership. "I'm so mad at Jim Wright and Tom Foley I don't want to talk to them, never mind negotiate with them in good faith," said GOP whip Trent Lott.[59] Cheney said that Wright was "a heavy-handed son of a bitch and he doesn't know any other way to operate, and he will do anything he can to win at any price. . . . It brings disrespect on the House itself."[60] As for Wright's timekeeping, a top House Republican said: "What the heck, they do that all the time, but the notion of John Mack dragging a member down into the well to change his vote, going through that whole exercise to get it passed, struck me as a bad piece of business."

Democrats noted that Wright had obeyed the letter of the rules. "What went on may have been different, but not unusual," said one leadership aide. "The message here is, if you want to change the place, go out and elect a majority."[61]

As always, Republicans had their differences. As a matter of principle, some opposed the tax increases in the reconciliation bill, while others were willing to consider them. In the short run, the confrontationists wanted to obstruct House business, while the responsible partners wanted to leave the episode behind. But they all resented Wright. When a lobbyist asked Cheney what message he could bring the speaker to restore good feelings, Cheney reportedly answered: "There isn't any message. We want his head."[62]

The Contra Vote of March 1988

In the late 1980s, the House had a series of votes on aid to the contras, the guerilla forces fighting the Marxist government of Nicaragua. One of these votes occurred in March 1988. Although a military-aid plan had recently gone down to defeat, Republicans sought again to bring such a proposal to the floor. The *Washington Post* reported: "Several times in the past week Wright has said that the House minority would have an opportunity to have its contra-aid plan voted on."[63] But the Rules Committee placed a Democratic plan for nonmilitary aid as an amendment to the Republican plan for military aid. Under this restrictive rule, members would vote on the Democratic plan first; if it passed, they would have no chance to vote on the Republican plan.

GOP Leader Michel believed that Wright had broken his commitment: "In over 30 years as a Member of this institution, I have kept my word. I expect others to do the same."[64] Cheney later noted the significance of Michel's comment: "Bob Michel is not a bombthrower, nor is he a man who uses strong language to express himself. It took a hell of a lot for him to go on the floor and say, in effect, that he thought the speaker had welshed on his word. It's that style of operation that we find offensive."[65]

Democrats belittled the complaints, saying that Republicans had already had their chance on military aid. And Wright denied Michel's charge, saying that he had merely promised an alternative under the rule, not a separate vote. Wright said: "I know that in his heart of hearts, Bob feels I have been fair."[66]

The Democratic amendment passed, but the bill was defeated on final passage by Democrats who opposed all aid and by Republicans who spurned what they saw as a "fig leaf." For the House, that outcome was less important than the mounting GOP animosity toward Wright. Republicans believed that the speaker had broken the rules, and that liberal pressure had pushed him into active support for the Nicaraguan regime.

Payback

The electoral deadlock of the 1980s, combined with the rise of ethics regulation and investigative journalism, helped spawn a new form of political combat, which Benjamin Ginsberg and Martin Shefter call RIP: Revelation, Investigation, Prosecution.[67] When a party or faction cannot defeat its opponents at the ballot box, it is now more likely to discredit them through charges of misconduct. In the early part of the decade, congressional Democrats had waged RIP battles against Republican targets such as Environmental Protection Agency Administrator Ann Gorsuch Burford and Labor Secretary Raymond J. Donovan. In the late 1980s, House Republicans got a chance to use RIP when newspapers raised questions about Speaker Wright's finances. As Gingrich told Suzanne Garment: "All we did was to universalize their selective standards . . . to say, 'If they're going to apply to Republicans, they'll have to apply to Democrats. If they apply to the executive branch, they apply to the legislature. If you want to write new rules, fine. But you can't have it both ways.' "[68]

The attack on Wright's ethics constituted a double payback: against the Democrats, for the ethics war against the administration; and against Wright himself, for his treatment of the House GOP. And apart from their desire for retribution, Gingrich and other confrontationists argued that Wright's alleged misdeeds were a symptom of a systemic corruption that resulted from the Democrats' long grip on congressional power.

During the summer of 1987, Gingrich started pressing for a House investigation of Wright. At first, many GOP members were wary. Tom Tauke said of the Gingrich effort: "Sometimes his style makes me feel uncomfortable. He has a tendency to jump in without being properly prepared, without thinking whether his action will help or hurt his long-term goals."[69] But Gingrich persisted and eventually won converts to his approach.

Two months after the 1988 contra vote, seventy-two House Republicans—including several members of the party leadership—signed a letter asking for a formal investigation of Wright by the ethics committee (formally called the Committee on Standards of Official Conduct). In September, Wright worsened his own woes by openly discussing CIA support for the contras. Michel and Cheney immediately filed a separate complaint against Wright, charging that he had disclosed classified information. A Michel aide said: "Bob was extremely upset about the issue. He considered it potentially more serious than anything in Gingrich's complaint or the Ethics Committee's charges."[70]

This complaint deepened the anger between the parties and fortified the GOP's confrontational wing. The following spring was a nightmare for House Democrats. Upon Cheney's selection as Defense Secretary, Gingrich harnessed anti-Wright sentiment within GOP ranks to win his upset victory as House GOP whip. The ethics committee unanimously approved a statement alleging ethics violations by Wright. (The statement focused on financial transactions and did not deal with Nicaragua.) In an unrelated incident, the *Washington Post* revealed that John Mack, the Wright aide who had helped reverse the 1987 reconciliation vote, was a convicted felon who had once committed a bloody assault against a young woman. The National Republican Congressional Committee issued a press release that said: "According to The Post, Mack is Speaker Wright's right-hand man. According to court records, that 'right hand' grabbed a hammer and slammed it into (his victim's) skull."[71]

New allegations against Wright surfaced in the press almost daily. Having failed to secure his base among House Democrats, he faced a wave of defections. With his support dwindling, he decided to resign. Meanwhile, Tony Coelho quit the House following news stories about his junk-bond dealings. Whatever the merits of the allegations, he knew that he was in for trouble. Republicans had been lusting for such ammunition for years.

Interparty conflict was not the only thing that brought down Wright and Coelho, because worries about their ethics were hardly confined to the House Republicans. Liberal magazines such as the *New Republic* and *Washington Monthly* had long before then questioned Wright's dealings.[72] Common Cause joined in the call for an investigation. And a book titled *Honest Graft* had cast Coelho's fundraising in an unflattering light.[73] After their long RIP war against Republican misconduct, Democrats had a tough time defending Wright and Coelho. At the 1988 convention, Coelho himself had scorned GOP ethics, pledging that Democrats would fight "the corporate cannibals on Wall Street."[74] (After resigning, he became an investment banker.)

Wright's farewell speech did little to heal the House. He said: "All of us in both political parties must resolve to bring this period of mindless cannibalism to an end."[75] Vin Weber said of the address: "I think it immediately played well, but it's not sitting well the day after. . . . It's sort of the big lie to say the [ethics] committee lynched Jim Wright." And Lynn Martin (R-Illinois) said that the Speaker reminded her of schoolchildren she had taught: "The dog ate my homework."[76]

When Thomas Foley succeeded Wright, Michel gave the GOP diagnosis of the House's problem: "Thirty-five years of uninterrupted power can act like a corrosive acid upon the restraints of civility and comity. Those who have been kings of the Hill for so long may forget that majority status is not a divine right—and minority status is not a permanent condition."[77]

The War Goes On

Ironically, the departure of Wright and Coelho brought the GOP no electoral benefit, for it robbed them of exhibits A and B in their case against the House Democrats. The new leadership team—Speaker Foley and Majority Leader Richard Gephardt—offered a more pleasing face to the public. House Republicans still welcomed the shift, because they thought they would get better treatment on the House floor; and in his early months, Foley seemed to justify their optimism by easing up on procedural warfare. The amity could not last. "Foley will learn," said Dan Glickman (D-Kansas), "there's a limit to fairness when the White House is controlled by the other party."[78]

Hints of conflict emerged as early as August 1989, when a Republican offered a motion to recommit a bill to the Appropriations Committee. Based upon the 1983 rule curbing limitation amendments, Foley ruled the motion out of order. Arguing that the rule did not apply to recommittal motions, Michel challenged the ruling—his first such step in his congressional career.

Republicans gradually concluded that the majority was continuing to tighten the procedural screws. In 1990, child care legislation came to the floor under a rule that allowed no Republican amendments and no motion to recommit. It also included a self-executing provision that automatically amended both the principal bill and a Democratic substitute. Michel's reaction is worth quoting at length:

> [T]he majority with its apparently craven fear of free debate has crafted a disgraceful rule that is a mockery of democratic procedure. Never before in the history of the House of Representatives has there been a rule that allows an amendment that simultaneously amends two different propositions at once. We have done so by unanimous consent, but never before in this House have we done it in the way the rule provides. . . . Mr. Speaker, if Mr. Gorbachev did something like this in the Soviet Union, we would be decrying his dictatorial ways. But we have no glasnost in this House. Do I have to say that we do not even have comity anymore? The Majority has turned this House into a den of inequity.[79]

Gerald Solomon (R-New York), soon to become ranking Republican on Rules, compared the rule with printed statements by Foley and Moakley that promised procedural fairness. "Even worse than that, if you want to know how bad this rule is . . ." he said, when Tom Downey (D-New York) interrupted, "How bad is it?" Solomon shot back: "I am going to tell you right now. You should not be a smart aleck about it because you ought to be serious about it."[80] He then drew large black X's through the Foley and Moakley statements.

The following year brought "the Congress from Hell." *Roll Call* reported that the House Bank had long given members free overdraft privileges on their checking accounts, or in effect, zero-interest loans. Other news organizations followed suit, and "congressional check-bouncing" became a national issue. Some of the confrontational Republicans urged disclosure of the overdrafters' names, hoping that the case would at last turn voters against the House Democrats. Others were not so confident. "You better be doggone sure you are pure yourself before you take on all this aura of purity," warned Michel.[81] As mentioned in Chapter 2, it turned out that dozens of Republicans had made overdrafts, and a number of them—including three members of the minority leadership—either stepped down or lost reelection bids. RIP cut both ways.

Several other administrative scandals broke open at the same time. Perhaps most disturbing for Republicans, a probe of the House Post Office revealed that House Postmaster Robert Rota had helped House Democrats keep tabs on their opposition. Whenever GOP members circulated a "Dear Republican Colleague" letter, Rota sent copies to Democratic aides and members, but he did not give "Dear Democratic Colleague" letters to Republicans.[82] Such revelations prompted management reforms, such as consolidation of administrative duties in a nonpartisan office of nonlegislative and financial services. Republicans argued that the overhaul was merely superficial, and that the institution's basic problem remained unsolved: two generations of Democratic control of the House.

The 1992 elections brought the federal government under unified Democratic control, so now the House majority could perhaps afford an occasional bow to the minority. On the other hand, even though a GOP majority was nowhere in sight, many Democrats fretted. Because the out-party usually wins seats in off-year elections, they worried that the 1994 election would allow the GOP to build on its 1992 gains. Many Democrats had seen their reelection margins slip in 1992, and they feared that their perceived vulnerability would earn them a place on Republican "hit lists." Remembering that GOP floor maneuvers in the late 1970s may have contributed to the Republican victories of 1980, House Democrats balked at granting more flexibility to the minority. Just as important, they could also remember the pain that the confrontational Republicans had caused them during the Jim Wright episode, so the rising influence of the GOP bombthrowers unnerved them further.

House Democrats started the new session with proposed rules changes that alarmed the GOP. At first, they planned to limit televised special orders, but the threat of disruptive Republican protests led them to defer the idea. They also sought to grant five nonvoting delegates—all Democrats—a vote in the Committee of the Whole. In Democratic eyes, the change was a noble effort to give a voice to disenfranchised American nationals. In Republican eyes, it was a maneuver to offset half of the GOP's ten-seat gain. Many House Republicans remembered that the last election that produced a Republican gain (1984) had also been followed by an alleged Democratic "theft," namely the McIntyre-McCloskey case. When the Republican critique won support from mainstream newspapers, the Democrats partially retreated. They offered a compromise procedure that effectively nullified the delegates' votes whenever they would change the outcome.

In April 1993, the Republicans had another bad flashback when the House voted on a rule for a bill concerning "expedited rescission" of federal spending. At the end of the roll call, the rule seemed to have lost. In an episode reminiscent of Wright's "long count," Speaker Foley then held the vote open for an additional thirteen minutes so that he could switch a couple of votes and reverse the outcome. Echoing Republican complaints, the *Wall Street Journal* decried the incident in an editorial titled "Jim Wright Returns."[83]

In this session, no open rule reached the House until May 5. During consideration of the budget reconciliation bill, Democrats refused to allow a vote on a GOP proposal to eliminate proposed tax increases and offset the forgone revenue with cuts in discretionary spending programs. The majority argued that such an amendment would have violated the Budget Enforcement Act. Republicans responded that the majority routinely waived budget laws, and enforced them in this instance only to limit GOP options.

Still, the House Republicans managed to score a few victories. On three occasions during the first session of the 103d Congress, they joined with dissident Democrats to defeat legislative rules.[84] And with the support of outside figures such as Ross Perot and Rush Limbaugh, they compelled the House to end the secrecy of the discharge petition, a procedure under which members can force floor action on bills mired in committee. Previously, the names of the members signing a discharge petition did not become public until it had reached the required total of 218. Now that the names would be public from the start, Republicans hoped voters would press lawmakers to sign discharge petitions for conservative measures that committees had blocked. Democrats feared that demagoguery would trump deliberation.

Meanwhile, personal relations between Republicans and Democrats remained bad. When Louise Slaughter (D-New York) sought to cut off a Republican colloquy on the House floor, Gerald Solomon responded: "You had better not do that, ma'am. You will regret that as long as you live. Who do you think you are?"[85] Solomon later apologized and withdrew the remark from the *Congressional Record*.

For sheer hatefulness, it would be hard to top a comment from William Clay (D-Missouri), who opposed the efforts of Gary Franks (R-Connecticut), the House's only black Republican, to take part in the Congressional Black Caucus. "I think he's a disgrace to the black race," Clay said. "I think it's a disgrace we would sit in the room and discuss civil rights with him."[86]

The war went on.

Procedure, Policy, and Politics

This protracted warfare has had several important consequences for House Republicans.

First, it has strengthened the confrontationists by undercutting the arguments of those who preach accommodation. Some of the latter contend that bombthrowing only makes matters worse by further antagonizing the liberal wing of the majority party. The confrontationists reply that the GOP experience under Foley proves the folly of accommodation.

Second, procedural maneuvers have deprived the GOP of opportunities to hold the majority accountable for its actions. In the late 1970s, Republicans could sometimes force the Democrats to take public stands on difficult issues. Such opportunities have largely vanished. On the 1993 reconciliation bill, for instance, Republicans could not obtain a separate vote on tax increases; Democrats could thus say they were voting for deficit reduction rather than higher taxes. (In 1981, House Democrats note, it was the *Republicans* who favored a single vote on reconciliation.) Notwithstanding their victory on discharge petitions, Republicans have had little success making a public issue out of congressional procedure, because few Americans care about such matters.

Third, the structure of debate has often unified Democrats and split Republicans. Again, the 1993 reconciliation bill provides an example. While barring the tax amendment, the majority on the Rules Committee did permit a vote on a GOP amendment to chop at popular entitlement programs. In supporting the amendment, Republicans had to go on record in favor of painful spending cuts without the balm of tax relief. The Republican defection rate on that vote exceeded the Democratic defection rate on final passage of the bill.

Time and again, the internal politics of the House has proved a source of deep frustration to House Republicans, who often can neither legislate nor score political points. Yet even if the majority showed more lenience to the minority, the House GOP's problems would continue. While procedural politics may loom large in the daily lives of House Republicans, it is but one part of a greater, more vexing puzzle.

Notes

1. Quoted in Kelly Marcavage and William A. Syers, eds., *Congress: Past, Present and Future* (Washington, D.C.: House Republican Research Committee, 1987), 15.

2. Quoted in Don Phillips, "Rep. Moakley's Mark on Rules; Chairman Blends Independence, Amicability," *Washington Post*, September 12, 1989, A19.

3. Quoted in John M. Barry, *The Ambition and the Power: The Rise and Fall of Jim Wright* (New York: Viking, 1989), 304.

4. Thomas E. Mann and Norman J. Ornstein, *Renewing Congress: A Second Report* (Washington, D.C.: Brookings, 1993), 64.

5. Charles O. Jones, *The Minority Party in Congress* (Boston: Little, Brown, 1970), 183.

6. For an historical overview of the rise of programmatic liberals, see James L. Sundquist, *Dynamics of the Party System: Alignment and Realignment of Political Parties in the United States*, rev. ed. (Washington, D.C.: Brookings, 1983), 262–68. On black voters' impact on southern Democratic House delegations, see David W. Rohde, *Parties and Leaders in the Postreform House* (Chicago: University of Chicago Press, 1991), 45–48.

7. Michael J. Malbin, "Factions and Incentives in Congress," *Public Interest* 86 (Winter 1987): 103.

8. Quoted in Norman Ornstein, "Minority Report," *Atlantic Monthly*, December 1985, 32.

9. Barbara Sinclair, *Majority Leadership in the U.S. House* (Baltimore: Johns Hopkins University Press, 1983), 4–5.

10. Roger H. Davidson and Walter J. Oleszek, *Congress Against Itself* (Bloomington: Indiana University Press, 1977), 267.

11. *Congressional Record*, daily ed., January 5, 1993, H24.

12. Katherine A. Hinckley, "Party Ratios on Congressional Committees

and Subcommittees, 80th-99th Congresses" (paper presented at the annual meeting of the American Political Science Association, Washington, D.C., August 27–31, 1986).

13. Quoted in Steven Komarow, "House Budget Committee OKs Spending Plan," Associated Press, May 8, 1986.

14. Steven S. Smith, *Call To Order: Floor Politics in the House and Senate* (Washington, D.C.: Brookings, 1989), 62–65.

15. Stanley Bach and Steven S. Smith, *Managing Uncertainty in the House of Representatives: Adaptation and Innovation in Special Rules* (Washington, D.C.: Brookings, 1988), 13–18.

16. Quoted in John J. Rhodes, *The Futile System: How to Unchain Congress and Make the System Work Again* (New York: EPM, 1976), 32–33.

17. Mann and Ornstein, *Renewing Congress: A Second Report*, 56.

18. Stanley Bach and Richard C. Sachs, "Legislation, Appropriations, and Limitations: The Effect of Procedural Change on Policy Choice" (paper presented at the annual meeting of the American Political Science Association, Atlanta, August 31–September 3, 1989).

19. *Congressional Record*. daily ed., January 5, 1993, H24.

20. Ibid.

21. Ibid., H24-H25.

22. Joint Committee on the Organization of Congress, *Operations of the Congress: Testimony of House and Senate Leaders*, 103d Congress, 1st sess., 1993 (S. Hrg. 103–10), 18–19.

23. Quoted in Marcavage and Syers, *Congress: Past, Present and Future*, 17.

24. Quoted in Richard L. Lyons, "On Capitol Hill," *Washington Post*, July 14, 1981, A4.

25. Eric M. Uslaner, "Comity in Context: Confrontation in Historical Perspective," *British Journal of Political Science*, 21 (January 1991): 45–77.

26. *Congressional Record*, daily ed., December 22, 1987, E4983-E4985. The article in question is: David Osborne, "Newt Gingrich: Shining Knight of the Post-Reagan Right," *Mother Jones*, November 1984, 15–20, 53.

27. Quoted in Don Phillips, "O'Neill: Mondale Must Attack 'Cold, Mean' Reagan," United Press International, July 19, 1984.

28. *Congressional Record* (bound), 97th Congress, 1st sess., June 25, 1981, 14077.

29. *Congressional Record* (bound), 97th Congress, 1st sess., June 26, 1981, 14562.

30. *Congressional Record*, daily ed., May 8, 1984, H3545.

31. *Congressional Record*, daily ed., May 8, 1984, H3553.

32. Tip O'Neill with William Novak, *Man of the House: The Life and Political Memoirs of Speaker Tip O'Neill* (New York: Random House, 1987), 354.

33. *Congressional Record*, daily ed., May 10, 1984, H3762.

34. Quoted in Craig Winneker, "Heard on the Hill," *Roll Call*, November 12, 1992, 1.

35. *Congressional Record*, daily ed., May 15, 1984, H3843.

36. Ibid.

37. Quoted in "Republicans Assail O'Neill; A Loss of Comity Is Feared," *New York Times*, May 18, 1984, A15.

38. Quoted in United Press International, May 21, 1984.

39. Democratic Congressional Campaign Committee press release, May 30, 1984.

40. Quoted in T. R. Reid, "It's 'Tip's Greatest Hits,' Electrifying a Closed House GOP Circuit," *Washington Post*, May 29, 1984, A3.

41. Quoted in United Press International, May 19, 1984.

42. Otis Pike, "Sneaky Tactics in House to Fill an Indiana Seat," *Newsday*, March 10, 1985, Ideas section, 7.

43. *Congressional Record* (bound), 99th Congress, 1st sess., March 4, 1985, 4281.

44. Quoted in Dave Doubrava, "Democrats Accused of Move to Steal Indiana House Seat," *Washington Times*, March 12, 1985, 2A.

45. "Paper Says Poll of Absentee Voters Shows McIntyre Would Win," Associated Press, May 3, 1985.

46. Quoted in Dan Balz, "Frustrations Embitter House GOP," *Washington Post*, April 29, 1985, A4.

47. *Congressional Record* (bound), 99th Congress, 1st sess., May 1, 1985, 9995.

48. Quoted in Margaret Shapiro, "The Toll of Turmoil," *Washington Post*, July 13, 1985, A5.

49. Democratic Study Group (United States House of Representatives), "An Honest Count . . . An Unwarranted Reaction" (Washington, D.C.: Democratic Study Group, 1985), Report 99-10.

50. Tony Coelho, "House Republicans' Own Medicine Has Bitter Taste" (letter), *Wall Street Journal*, May 17, 1985, 25.

51. Quoted in Balz, "Frustrations," A4.

52. Ibid.

53. Lungren statement in *Congressional Record* (bound), 99th Congress, 1st sess., June 27, 1985, 17894.

54. Quoted in John M. Barry, "The Man of the House," *New York Times Magazine*, November 23, 1986, 60.

55. Fred Barnes, "Raging Representatives," *The New Republic*, June 3, 1985, 9.

56. Barbara Sinclair, "The Evolution of Party Leadership in the Modern House," in *The Atomistic Congress: An Interpretation of Congressional Change*, ed. Allen D. Hertzke and Ronald M. Peters, Jr. (Armonk, N.Y.: M. E. Sharpe, 1992), 285.

57. *Congressional Record*, daily ed., October 29, 1987, H9130–31.

58. *Congressional Record*, daily ed., October 29, 1987, H9157.

59. Quoted in Laurence McQuillan, "House Tax Vote Stirs Bitterness," Reuters, October 30, 1987.

60. Quoted in James A. Barnes, "Partisanship," *National Journal*, November 7, 1987, 2825.

61. Ibid.

62. Quoted in John M. Barry, "Games Congressmen Play," *New York Times Magazine*, May 13, 1990, 85.

63. Tom Kenworthy, "GOP Opposes Contra Aid Voting Plan; House to Consider Democrats' Bill First," *Washington Post*, March 2, 1988, A4.

64. *Congressional Record*, daily ed., March 3, 1988, H644.

65. Quoted in Cheryl Arvidson, "Wright Rankles GOP Leader," *Dallas Times-Herald*, May 20, 1988, A12.

66. Quoted in Jonathan Fuerbringer, "A House Divided by Political Rancor," *New York Times*, March 16, 1988, A22.

67. Benjamin Ginsberg and Martin Shefter, *Politics by Other Means: The Declining Importance of Elections in America* (New York: Basic, 1990), 26–31.

68. Quoted in Suzanne Garment, *Scandal: The Culture of Mistrust in American Politics* (New York: Random House/Times Books, 1991), 232.

69. Quoted in John E. Yang, "Gingrich's Fiery Fight to Prove Wright Is Wrong Has House GOP Colleagues Scurrying for Cover," *Wall Street Journal*, May 20, 1988, 52.

70. Quoted in Richard E. Cohen, "Fall From Power," *National Journal*, August 19, 1989, 2087.

71. Quoted in Michael Oreskes, "Wright Assistant Has Criminal Past," *New York Times*, May 5, 1989, A14.

72. Paul West, "The Wright Stuff," *New Republic*, October 14, 1985, 22–25; Steven Waldman, "The Man Who Would Be Speaker," *Washington Monthly*, March 1986, 28–37.

73. Brooks Jackson, *Honest Graft: Big Money and the American Political Process* (New York: Knopf, 1988).

74. Democratic National Committee, *Official Proceedings of the 1988 Democratic National Convention*. (Washington, D.C.: Democratic National Committee, 1988), 302.

75. *Congressional Record*, daily ed., May 31, 1989, H2247.

76. Quoted in Don Phillips, "Republicans Bridle at Wright Speech; GOP Urges Clearer Rules, Not Retribution Over Speaker's Demise," *Washington Post*, June 2, 1989, A6.

77. *Congressional Record*, daily ed., June 6, 1989, H2283.

78. Quoted in Barry, "Games Congressmen Play," 85.

79. *Congressional Record*, daily ed., March 29, 1990, H1254.

80. *Congressional Record*, daily ed., March 29, 1990, H1248.

81. Quoted in Clifford Krauss, "Success Strains GOP: House Leadership Split," *New York Times*, March 20, 1992, A11.

82. Glenn R. Simpson, "Rota Mailed 'Dear Colleagues' to Scores of Favored Lobbyists," *Roll Call*, July 27, 1992, 1, 18.

83. "Jim Wright Returns" (editorial), *Wall Street Journal*, April 30, 1993, A10.

84. Timothy J. Burger, "Number of Rules Defeated This Session Is Up Sharply," *Roll Call*, December 6, 1993, 10–11.

85. "New Yorker to New Yorker: Before and After," *Roll Call*, March 29, 1993, 40.

86. Quoted in Kenneth J. Cooper, "The Black Caucus's Odd Man In," *Washington Post*, September 1, 1993, C1.

Chapter 5

Interests, Institutions, Ideas, and Individuals

The action of the past three chapters has taken place largely within a few hundred yards of the Capitol dome. We have seen how House Republicans have dealt with their plight, both in internal organization and in relations with House Democrats. Now that we have looked at the consequences of minority status, we turn to causes and possible cures.

Are House Republicans a minority because they are fools, or because House Democrats are knaves? Among political scientists, Gary Jacobson holds that Republicans lose because they field weak candidates on the wrong side of the issues, while Morris Fiorina places more emphasis on "structural" causes such as the incumbency advantage.[1] Among House Republicans, some promote a grand "national" strategy, while others stress the seat-by-seat trench warfare of local politics.

In these debates, each side has something to offer. Political scientists and politicians have been not so much wrong as incomplete in their discussions of the House Republicans' minority status. Most analyses overlook the linkages between structural and political explanations. If Republicans have a hard time coordinating their campaign messages or running nationwide recruitment drives, the reason lies not just in shortsighted individuals, but in a constitutional system that hampers such efforts. Academic and practical studies of congressional elections have also slighted the role of ideas and political culture in setting the context for political campaigns.

Analyses of consequences, causes and cures are interlocked, so we need an explanation that looks outside Capitol Hill and relates the problem's elements to one another. The metaphor of a Rubik's Cube^(TM) furnishes a good starting point. The challenge behind this popular yet baffling three-dimensional puzzle is to align all similarly colored squares on the same sides of the cube. Just as you finish twisting the puzzle to get one side all of a color, you usually find that you have disarranged all the other sides. Like a Rubik's Cube, the House GOP's quandary is maddeningly intricate. And compounding this predicament are the many hands grabbing at the "cube": that is, the Republicans who proffer conflicting solutions and the Democrats who try to block them.

Before getting carried away with this image, we must make some qualifications. Political scientists like to use typologies and other devices that sort things into tidy boxes. These devices have pitfalls. They imply, often inaccurately, that causes are similar or that they contribute equally to the object of study. They also suggest an inevitability that one seldom finds in politics. Although these caveats apply with special force to multidimensional matrices, such as a Rubik's Cube, this image has a great advantage: it reveals the shortcomings of one-dimensional diagnoses and prescriptions. After all, nobody can solve the puzzle by looking at only one side of the cube.

Widening the Scope of Analysis

Broader explanations of complex political phenomena have a distinguished ancestry. More than a century and a half ago, Tocqueville said that a "new political science is needed for a world itself quite new."[2] He told students of American politics to search beneath and above the narrow definition of politics.

Tocqueville analyzed liberal democracy in America by using a three-part framework: physical circumstances, laws, and mores. Physical circumstances included the land's breadth and bounty; the vast oceans separating the United States from other nations; and "the social state," including differences in social and economic interests. Tocqueville's examination of laws encompassed the republic's constitution and statutes as well as "secondary powers" such as the press, political parties, and other political associations. Most important, "mores" consisted of the nation's political culture: its "habits of the heart," "opinions," "the sum of ideas," and indeed, "the whole moral and intellectual state of a people."[3]

In a famous passage, Tocqueville concluded that the "laws contribute more to the maintenance of the democratic republic in the United

States than do the physical circumstances of the country, and mores do more than the laws.''[4] In the 1920s, political scientist Pendleton Herring followed Tocqueville's path when he said that the parties' difficulty in carrying out coherent programs reflected "the structure of the government" and "changes that have occurred in fields not directly connected with politics."[5] In accounting for the absence of programmatic parties, Herring singled out institutional forces such as the separation of powers, and sociological developments such as divisions between cities and rural areas. A half century later, James W. Ceaser put the conditions for party strength into four categories: doctrinal, legal, environmental, and political.[6]

Our Rubik's Cube metaphor builds on the insights of Herring and Ceaser.[7] The roles of interests, institutions, and ideas correspond to the cube's three dimensions, and the actions of individuals constitute the hands twisting the cube.

Interests

At least since Madison, political scientists have weighed the role of "various and interfering interests."[8] For our purposes, "interests"

Figure 5-1
The House GOP's Puzzle

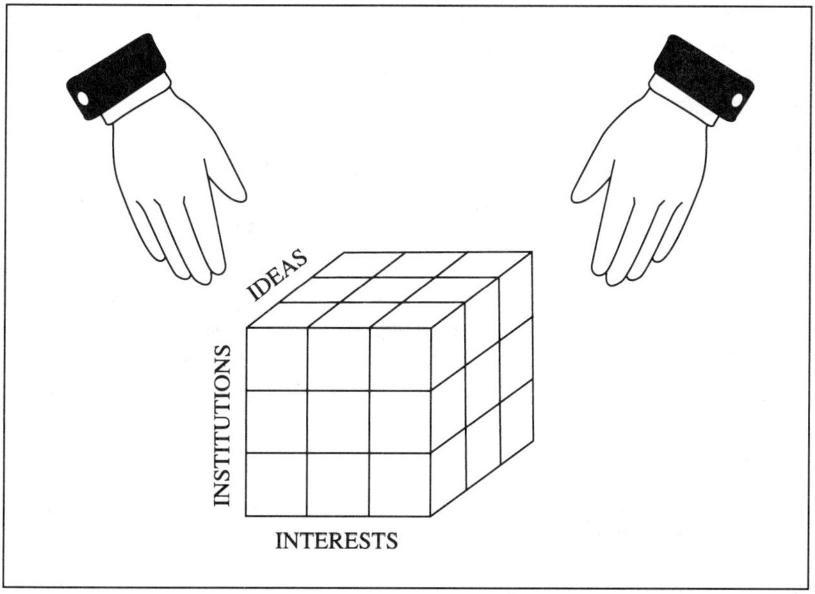

comprise the social, demographic, and economic concerns that undergird much of American politics. Taken as a whole, these interests are neither fixed nor all-powerful: people often change their minds about what they want for themselves, and they sometimes put the country's good ahead of their own. Since politics is not reducible to economics, the competition of ideas may be as important as the struggle among interests. Still, the politics of interest explains a great deal about Congress. And during the 1980s and early 1990s, it whipsawed the House Republicans in several ways.

Economic interests affect congressional voting. Recessions generally inflate the midterm losses of the party holding the White House, and the deep downturn of 1982 cost the House GOP twenty-six seats, or one-seventh of its membership. The economy then recovered and moved into the longest peacetime expansion in American history. House Republicans, however, made only small gains in 1984 and posted net losses in the next three elections. If they got the punishment for bad times, why did they get so little reward for good times?

For one thing, they ran afoul of what Tocqueville called America's "passion for equality" and what Madison identified as the most durable source of faction: "the various and unequal distribution of property."[9] Prosperity neither touched every corner of society nor did it turn every indicator in the right direction. Between 1982 and 1989, the poverty rate stayed high and real average weekly earnings actually dropped.[10] Correctly or incorrectly, millions of Americans perceived rising inequality. Voters think Democrats do better than Republicans at ensuring "fairness," so when these concerns come to the fore, Democrats gain.[11] Another trend aiding Democrats at the expense of House Republicans has been the diversification of interest-group politics. In the wake of World War II, America was a "big unit" society: big government, big business, big labor.[12] Voters and analysts alike saw American politics as the management of large interest blocs. The GOP did well during this period; in fact, the last time the GOP won an absolute majority of the vote in a House election was 1946, the year after the war's end. In recent decades, the old-bloc politics has weakened as changes in technology, society, and the economy have:

• Spawned completely new industries, such as biotechnology;

• Rearranged the country's ethnic makeup, with the number of Latinos rising 53 percent during the 1980s alone.[13]

• Fragmented existing interests, such as the health-care industry, which now includes health maintenance organizations, preferred provider organizations, and other diverse elements;

• Galvanized previously unorganized interests, such as homosexuals and Christian fundamentalists.

One rough measure of this change consists of the total number of nonprofit associations, which increased from 14,726 in 1980 to 22,455 in 1992.[14] Historically the party of "special interests" and "cultural diversity," the Democrats have shown great skill at working this segmented marketplace. Some House Democrats champion semiconductor makers, while others fight for oil drillers, gays, hunters, dairy farmers, Latinos, police officers, and investment bankers. Many continue to court organized labor, whose purported death is an exaggeration. Manufacturing-industry unions, which once provided Democrats with massive organizational strength, did suffer a net loss of one and a half million members between 1983 and 1992. But government-employee unions gained more than 900,000 members during the same period.[15] These unions typically give more than 90 percent of their PAC contributions to Democrats, and they supply the party with cadres of articulate activists in every corner of the country.[16]

During his time as chair of the Democratic Congressional Campaign Committee, Tony Coelho ingeniously sought to match PACs with Democratic candidates who had congenial backgrounds or philosophies. According to the DCCC's political director, the staff made sales calls to corporate PAC managers: "We would go in there with biographies and say, 'Well, look, he's owned his own Pizza Hut.' "[17] Lobbyists referred to Coelho's PAC receptions as "meat markets."

Despite internal factionalism, the House Republicans have a narrower electoral base, and their "permanent minority" status has hampered efforts to attract support from organized interests. One southern Republican complained: "The stacking of Ways and Means, Appropriations and Rules insures that business will support the Democrats."

Officeholders, candidates, and potential candidates make up an important interest category of their own. The rise of what Alan Ehrenhalt calls the "new governing class" puts House Republicans at a strategic disadvantage.[18] That is, bright young Republicans go into business while bright young Democrats go into politics; the Democrats thus field a stronger "farm team." Echoing this argument, one committee ranking member said that House Republicans had "a genetic defect" in their inability to run the professional candidates that House Democrats promote. Early in the 1992 cycle, an eastern moderate told us: "The business of Republicans is business. For Democrats, it's politics." Eleven months later, this member lost his seat to a forty-two-year-old Democratic state legislator who had first sought office three years after graduating from a law school in Washington, D.C.

Another element of the political environment is the baby boomers' "therapeutic culture," which demands greater opportunities for participation in public life.[19] Modern technology supplies a way to meet this demand. During the 1992 elections, radio talk show hosts and Ross Perot popularized the "electronic town hall," inviting high-tech participation by voters and perhaps further eroding the notion of representation. Bill Clinton thrived in this atmosphere, as did many House Democrats in their districts.

Among House Republicans, the shift to the confrontational wing has meant more emphasis on media politics. Whereas many conservative Republicans used to shun the press because of its purported liberal bias, the media of the 1990s gave them direct access to certain audiences. COS pioneered the use of special orders to reach C-SPAN viewers and rally Republican troops. During the Reagan administration, Gingrich said: "Television communicates morale. For example, people in the executive branch will watch their champions fight on a topic. That builds the morale of the people in the executive branch so they will take more risks."[20] Now Republicans have access to a conservative cable network, National Empowerment Television. Rush Limbaugh has aided the Republicans by reprinting House GOP Conference material in his newsletter, and letting Robert Dornan (R-California) serve as a substitute host on his radio program.

When choosing congressional leaders, both parties increasingly consider media skills. Among Democrats, Richard Gephardt rose to the majority leadership in part because of his cool, "mediagenic" demeanor, a sharp contrast to Jim Wright's florid style. Among Republicans, Dick Cheney's unchallenged advance through the leadership was fostered by the *gravitas* that he projected through the television screen.

Institutions

Congress is more than the sum of its parts, and institutional pressures can color how lawmakers see their self-interest.[21] The reelection motive will induce them to heed their constituents' wants, but Congress' internal incentives can harness their ambitions to loftier goals.[22] Those incentives come from the committee and party systems, which both affect how members gain power on the Hill: they can rise by looking beyond their hometown interests.

New laws and rules, however, can alter members' incentives. Campaign finance reforms may have altered the balance between party leaders and their followers. Expanded perquisites of office may tip the balance between party loyalty and constituent service. Such innovations may have made members more independent of party leaders and presidents, and more dependent on contributors and constituents. Either way, institutions provide part of the context for leadership.

Institutions also influence the relative strength of parties. Madison said that our constitutional structure would curb factions, groups driven by passions or interests "adverse to the rights of other citizens, or to the permanent and aggregate interests of the community."[23] Although he feared that parties could become factious, he also believed that "an extinction of parties necessarily implies either a universal alarm for the public safety, or an absolute extinction of liberty."[24] The Founders wanted neither to ban parties nor grant them official status, but to check and control them.[25] They wanted a nation big enough to embrace a variety of interests, so it would be "less probable that a majority of the whole will have a common motive to invade the rights of other citizens."[26] Although parties have sometimes established dominance within a legislative chamber, the system has thwarted top-to-bottom "responsible" parties on the European model.

The institutions of government have also complicated the life of the parties. A national party can scarcely act as a well-oiled machine so long as its leaders—in the White House, the Senate, the House of Representatives, and the states—all have separate constituencies and power bases. In Woodrow Wilson's words, American parties "are like armies without officers, engaged upon a campaign which has no great cause at its back. Their names and traditions, not their hopes and policy, keep them together."[27]

Wilson's observation applies across both parties, but it has deeper significance for the House Republicans. They have to upset the status quo, whereas the majority benefits from a quiet battlefield. To continue with the martial analogy, one may cite the great military theorist Carl von Clausewitz: "It is easier to hold ground than to take it. . . . Any omission of attack—whether from bad judgment, fear or indolence—accrues to the defenders' benefit."[28]

Especially when an army fights steep odds, it needs cohesion. But this cohesion is worn down by what Clausewitz called *friction*: communication failures, red tape, internal rivalries, and the countless other problems that hinder smooth operations. An army—or a political party—may seem basically simple, but "none of its components is of one piece: each part is composed of individuals, every one of whom retains his potential of friction [and] the least important of whom may chance to delay things or somehow make them go wrong."[29]

The big problem for a national political strategy is that such friction lies in the very bones of our constitutional structure.

Take, for instance, the "recipe for Republicans" offered by political scientist Thomas Mann: improving party image and identification, heightening partisan differences, fielding good challengers and open-seat candidates, making further southern inroads, blocking gerrymanders, and losing the White House (thus escaping the midterm drag of the 1980s).[30] All of these ingredients make sense, yet because of our fragmented system, none lies entirely within the power of the House Republicans, who encounter great friction when seeking the cooperation of other elements of the party. Said Ed Rollins:

> I think what's happened, unfortunately, is that no one but this committee [NRCC] cares about congressional races. The national committee has other priorities. The state parties have other priorities, but everybody cares about a U.S. Senate race, everybody cares about a governor's race, everybody cares about legislative races. . . . Nobody ever says, 'The most important thing this cycle is to elect Republicans to the House.' It's always kind of an afterthought.[31]

For a clearer picture of the GOP's institutional frustrations, consider four major features of American political architecture: federalism, the separation of powers, bicameralism, and the House's own structure.

Federalism

House Democrats like to tell their GOP colleagues: "Quit complaining about being in the minority. Just go out and run better candidates." This taunt torments the GOP leaders because they want to run better candidates but have little ability to do so. National party organizations have no legal authority to place candidates on any ballot, and must instead rely on state and local parties, as well as the candidates themselves. While NRCC can try to identify and encourage potential candidates, its fitful efforts have yielded disappointing harvests. National party bureaucrats can seldom gain a firm knowledge of potential contenders and how they might match their constituencies. Local party organizations know more about likely candidates, but as Rollins suggested, they spend less effort on House races than elections for state and local office. After all, winning a race for county executive brings more tangible partisan rewards (e.g., patronage jobs) than winning a congressional election.[32] Just as national party organizations lack the means to choose good House candidates, local organizations lack the motive.

During the 1980s, local party organizations continued their long-term decline, which hurt Republicans more than Democrats. With their strongholds in state and local government and their support among teachers' unions and other extensive interest groups, Democrats were in a better position to reach voters without relying on the traditional party apparatus. The national GOP came up short in its effort to revive its local structure.[33] Washington-based operatives approached party development as a purely mechanical problem of supplying technical know-how to the provinces, much as Peace Corps volunteers would teach personal hygiene to Third World peasants. In the absence of an inspiring message, the GOP sparked little enthusiasm among volunteers.

State and local officials also have an issue perspective that diverges from that of national lawmakers. They do not handle the national security matters that intrigue Washingtonians; instead they must stick to dreary domestic topics such as solid waste disposal. And they must labor under balanced-budget rules and other fiscal constraints that do not apply to Capitol Hill. So when Washington-based party strategists seek to sound a consistent party message, discordant notes may come from Springfield or Sacramento.

Separation of Powers

Just as the Founders intended, the separation of powers remains a strong determinant of congressional behavior.[34] Authority coincides with capacity, allowing the three branches to check one another, while meeting their constitutional duties.

At the same time, the separation of powers hinders party unity.[35] Whereas a national strategy to win the House calls for single-mindedness and audacity, the president's constitutional position tends to summon broad-mindedness and compromise. As Vin Weber (R-Minnesota) put it: "What is good for the president may well be good for the country, but it is not necessarily good for congressional Republicans."[36] Minority status makes friction even more likely. Said Jerry Lewis (R-California): "As for influencing what happens inside the House, we have just enough votes to be irresponsible."[37]

During Republican administrations, the president and the national party committee may grate against the congressional campaign committee. According to reporter Bill Whalen: "The drive down Pennsylvania Avenue from NRCC headquarters to the White House is not unlike embarking on a plane from Madrid and landing in Lisbon. The inhabitants may look alike, they certainly sound alike, but they speak different languages."[38] Former Republican National Committee chairman Frank Fahrenkopf recalled "a real conflict of interest" in the 1972 campaign, where Nixon insisted on pumping up turnout among conservative Democrats, who would vote for their party's candidates below the presidential level. According to Ed Rollins, Nixon's "insistence on turning out every Democrat who might vote for him cost us a tremendous number of seats in the California Legislature and the congressional delegation. It put us behind the eight-ball for the whole decade."[39]

Such friction not only muddies the party message, but hurts party morale. After the Reagan landslide of 1984, the House GOP troops brooded over their paltry gains. Republican Leader Michel blamed the Reagan camp's obsession with boosting the president's own vote:

> As good a communicator as the president is, he really never, in my opinion, enjoined that issue of what it really means to have the numbers in the House. . . . Shoot, you don't need but three sentences or four (in campaign appearances) but you've got to pound 'em hard. . . . I've always said that presidents don't (have to) win by sixty and seventy percent. Here the son of a buck ended up with fifty-nine percent and you bring in fifteen seats. I don't think people should expect too many victories (for Reagan's program) when we are still that far behind.[40]

Bicameralism

According to Madison, bicameralism renders the House and Senate, "by different principles of action and different modes of election, as little connected with each other as the nature of their common functions and their common dependence on the society will admit."[41] This idea shapes the relationship between House and Senate party leaders: coordination is the exception rather than the rule.[42]

One source of friction lies hidden in plain sight. House members, with their two-year term, must always watch the political calendar, but only one-third of Senate terms expire in any election year. Senators may not always act as farsighted solons, but they face less political pressure to gain short-run advantage.

Just as important, a party may have a majority in one chamber and a minority in the other. In this case, philosophical kinship will often give way to the conflict between a majority outlook that emphasizes governing, and a minority outlook that emphasizes grandstanding. This is what happened to congressional Republicans between 1981 and 1987. In a 1984 interview, Bob Dole (R-Kansas) explained: "In the Senate, where we have a majority, we have less freedom to run around and stake out positions of our own. We're supporting the president's position; we have to think of votes. . . . While we're passing the legislation, they're [House Republicans] looking around for new ideas."[43] In 1985, then-Senator Dan Quayle put a positive spin on the same idea: "They are conducting the intellectual work of the Republican Party. I wish we had the time for that over here."[44] Sherwood Boehlert (R-New York) thought that such attitudes were scarce among senators: "Some of them don't acknowledge that we exist over here. A lot of them act as if the Senate has been to the mountain and that they have seen the truth."[45] In reaction to this sentiment, Dole reportedly told House GOP leaders: "We all know that you all think we are jerks."[46]

The Character of the House

"We thought we could change the country," Connie Mack (R-Florida) told Sidney Milkis about COS hopes, "but this place [the House] is designed to ensure that doesn't happen."[47] The GOP has little say over floor procedures because of a Rules Committee run by the Democrats. In a body such as the House, most of the instruments of internal influence—staff allotments, assignments of bills to committee—belong to the majority party. Unlike the Senate, where even a single member can use dilatory tactics to extract legislative concessions, the House offers few points of leverage to the opposition. Gerald Solomon, the House Republicans' ranking member on the Rules Committee, argued that Democratic domination has degenerated into "minority tyranny": though liberals make up a majority of the Democratic caucus, they constitute a minority of the whole House. By compelling conservative Democrats to side with them on procedural votes, they subvert true majority rule with abuse of restrictive rules.

The Constitution complicates GOP calculations by providing for complex rather than simple majority rule. Because members of the minority party can sometimes take part in policymaking, they face the choice of playing "government or opposition." Some seek ideological goals using the vehicle of party organization. As Newt Gingrich said: "We should prefer comity with the voters to comity with the House Democrats." Other members pursue policy goals within the committee system. Although Willis Gradison (R-Ohio) faced frustrations on the Budget Committee, he made serious contributions to health care policy on the Ways and Means Committee. During our interview, Gradison hinted that the House GOP's inability to influence committees is sometimes a "self-fulfilling prophecy."

Party activism is tempered by constituency pressure as well as committee politics. The local basis of House elections amplifies the localism that frustrates "progressive" reformers. Unlike a parliament, whose members seldom have deep roots in their constituencies, the U.S. House of Representatives is "so constituted as to support in the members an habitual recollection of their dependence on the people."[48] As James W. Ceaser put it: "Congressional elections work from the bottom up, giving heavy emphasis to concrete interests and emphasizing particulars." They encourage "pragmatic considerations over broader ideological patterns of thinking."[49]

The growth of government has intensified House localism by shifting Congress' focus from deliberation to representation.[50] Bigger bureaucracies mean more constituent problems to solve and more opportunities to claim credit for securing constituent benefits, so members ensure reelection by legislating less and playing ombudsman more. Staffing trends offer one sign of this tendency: over time, members have devoted a greater share of Washington-based staff to constituent activities.[51]

Some might see television as a counterweight to localism. Although the House Republicans find attentive audiences in the "alternative media" discussed earlier, their main hope of influencing the national agenda still rests with the traditional news media. As a complex institution, however, the House does not lend itself to clear and sustained media coverage. A conservative California Republican pointed out that local newspapers seldom publish the partisan breakdown of House votes, "so the public does not learn the difference between the parties." Robert Michel said, "the things that don't happen in the House can change the nature of a vote. The press is equipped to report on barking dogs, but not on dogs that don't bark."[52] He concluded that the media cover the House "in brief flashes of lightning, a scandal here followed a long time later by a hearing there, and the rest is silence and darkness."[53]

Systematic studies of the news media support Michel's observation: the House receives spotty press coverage, and the Senate gets more than the House.[54] So no matter how many "special order" speeches House Republicans may deliver, no matter how many rhetorical points they win during floor debate, little of their message will reach the general electorate.

Ideas

The third condition of party strength is the role of ideas. Tocqueville saw a nation's *moeurs* or political culture as a more fundamental condition for its political life than either physical circumstances or laws. The political culture includes the governing doctrines held by elite or public opinion. These doctrines include attitudes toward political parties in general, and the Democratic and Republican parties in particular.

Ideas matter in their own right, not just as packaging for interests. Self-government, meaning government by "reflection and choice" rather than "accident and force," only makes sense if deliberation and persuasion can move individuals to act.[55] For good or ill, FDR's liberalism and Reagan's conservatism both shaped our politics by shaping the government and the economy. Both the rise and fall of the New Deal public philosophy, and the GOP's struggle to devise an alternative, have influenced the parties' fortunes in the House.

Ideas have split the House Republicans. In addition to the division between moderates and conservatives, the House GOP has had to contend with the perennial conflict between outsiders and insiders, a tension as old as the republic itself. In the late 1980s and early 1990s, as the voters scorned insiderism, the outsiders seemed to gain the upper hand within the House GOP conference. And yet outsiderism was not moving House Republicans toward a majority. Institutional forces pulled many of them toward the "inside" politics of committee work and constituency service, and even some vocal "outsiders" had gradually acquired the trappings of "insiders." In 1992, Gingrich nearly lost his seat to a primary challenger who mocked him for taking government perquisites, such as a Lincoln Town Car with driver.[56] And in the general election of that year, voters doubted the "outsider" status of a party that had occupied the White House for twenty of the past twenty-four years.

Of the new House members elected in 1992, 70 percent had held elective office.[57] The victory of professionals in an outsider's year is not as paradoxical as it may seem. Someone with long experience in state or local politics can still plausibly run against the Washington establishment: witness Jimmy Carter in 1976, Ronald Reagan in 1980 and Bill Clinton in 1992. A cynic could also speculate that it takes a great deal of professionalism to play the role of an amateur.

In either case, the results jibe with Alan Ehrenhalt's *United States of Ambition*, which documents the professionalization of politics. Although both parties had greater success than before in fielding experienced candidates, the Democrats held onto their edge, which we described earlier in this chapter. About two-thirds of Democratic open-seat candidates had elective experience, compared with half of the Republicans.[58] According to Ehrenhalt, Democratic and Republican ideas on the role of government have influenced the supply of experienced candidates. The Democratic Party celebrates government, so it has become the natural home of ambitious young people who seek public careers. The Republican Party, whether one calls it antigovernment or pro-limited-government, has a tougher time persuading its adherents to join the government. A junior Republican from the Midwest concurred: "Generally, it is difficult to find party activists who have a 'less government is better' philosophy to dedicate their lives to government service. Hence, we have not always fielded our best candidates and very seldom [fielded] good young ones who could build seniority."

Similarly, the broad sweep of public ideas helps explain Jacobson's argument that House Republicans remain in the minority because they are wrong on the issues. In an era of ticket-splitting, different issues have affected elections for Congress and the White House. Although national security and social issues helped the GOP win a majority of presidential races between 1948 and 1988, "bread and butter" issues generally helped the Democrats in congressional elections. Despite some fluctuations on taxes and other issues, the voters generally came to accept the broad goals of the welfare state (e.g., easing poverty, providing economic security for the elderly, ensuring equality of educational opportunity), which they associated more with Democrats than with Republicans.

During the 1980s, public opinion on domestic policy arguably drifted leftward in several ways.[59] For instance, the share of people saying that we were spending too much on the problems of the big cities declined from 21 percent in 1980 to 10 percent in 1988, while the percentage saying we were spending too little went up from 40 to 46 percent.[60] Ironically, this shift may well have come in reaction to the Reagan presidency: at least some Americans thought that he had gone far enough in curbing social spending.

The change in public opinion also reflected changes in elite opinion. While the Zeitgeist had once smiled upon conservative critiques of big government, now it favored condemnations of the "decade of greed." Despite serious questions about the quality of its research, Kevin Phillips's *The Politics of Rich and Poor* colored journalistic and academic views of the 1980s.[61] This book, along with the countless articles it inspired, called attention to bad trends (e.g., falling real wages) while slighting good ones, such as the post-1985 plunge in real tax rates for poor families. And as Christopher DeMuth wrote in 1988, even business "does not have the same enthusiasm for getting government off its back."[62] The former Reagan official, who now heads the American Enterprise Institute, continued: "The new issues, like corporate governance and hostile takeovers, split the business and the financial community. And business is badly divided over free trade versus protectionism."[63]

In response to a questionnaire, one House Republican wrote us a glum assessment of the climate of opinion:

As long as the American people have the attitude that government spending is good as long as it benefits them, the problem will continue. Democrats promise the moon, and eventually they'll deliver the moon if it costs taxpayers enough. Of course this procedure will be the ruination of America, but as long as the giveaway folks run government, ruination is just around the corner. . . . This is an exercise in total futility. Americans love to vote for the guy or gal who promises the most. This won't change until Americans decide there's no such thing as a free lunch.

Another point of view may hold more hope: that it is possible to achieve the goals of the New Deal welfare state through means that stress decentralization and market forces. According to this view, Republicans can win not by outbidding the Democrats on bigger government, but by offering a message of leaner, more effective government. Through the Bush administration, however, House Republicans were not yet rallying around such a philosophy. In the words of a Republican political consultant:

> The GOP problem, therefore, is that it lacks all value cohesion. All the GOP ever agrees upon are flag-waving, symbolic issues of protest. There is no legitimate legislative proposal besides defense spending. . . . The House Republicans really don't stand for anything, and as a result, they cannot focus on a common purpose, only frustrating the majority.

They were torn by intellectual forces as well as political ones. The conservative movement, which had surged in the late 1970s, was now splintered among paleoconservatives and neoconservatives, interventionists and neoisolationists, libertarians and "the religious right."[64] The disagreements deepened after the fall of the Berlin Wall. A passage from an article by Patrick Buchanan suggests the bitterness of such disputes: "With the unifying issue of anti-communism fading, the deep disagreements between neo-cons and traditional conservatives are surfacing. And the time to split the blanket has probably arrived. Before true conservatives can ever take back the country, they are first going to have to take back their movement."[65]

Few congressional Republicans were prepared to assume intellectual leadership in resolving this family feud. According to the head of one think tank: "Some Republicans latch onto ideas the way skateboarders latch on to buses: they hang on for a while and then let go." One moderate Republican singled out Newt Gingrich for the following barb: "Newt is not a detail person, rather he's a Doctor of Philosophy, a big picture man. . . . He's a butterfly. He sees other flowers and flutters away. He likes to pretend he's Rousseau or Emerson." Gingrich would argue that the "big picture" is important, and that the party must replace its old language of dour austerity with a new language of hope and opportunity. His supporters also note that he has indeed been consistent on major issues such as taxation, and that he has worked to unify ideological factions.

Whatever the case may be, this example illustrates how the politics of ideas overlaps with the politics of individuals.

Individuals

The fourth and final cause is politics narrowly defined: individuals and their actions, the subjects of the morning papers and the evening news.

Individuals are not simply molded by their environment; they can in turn shape it within limits defined by existing interests, institutions, and ideas. Individuals matter, especially leaders who can define a party's principles. Leaders can persuade voters and fellow politicians to follow by appealing to their interests, passions, and opinions. Consider three groups of individuals: House Republicans, House Democrats, and the members of the executive branch.

House Republicans. After the Reagan years, House Republicans lost some formidable leaders as permanent minority status diminished the value of leadership spots and made other career options more tempting. Jack Kemp left the Conference chair to seek the White House. Trent Lott gave up the second-highest House GOP office to become junior senator from Mississippi. And his successor as whip, Dick Cheney, resigned when President Bush asked him to serve as Defense Secretary. Cheney's departure was a sharp blow: among House Republicans, he had the greatest national stature and the greatest capacity to work with the party's warring factions. Moderates respected his service as President Ford's chief of staff, and conservatives liked his staunchly Reaganite voting record. Responsible partners admired his patient mastery of public policy, and bombthrowers cheered his occasional—but powerful—assaults against the House Democrats.

During interviews in 1991, a number of members mentioned Vin Weber as a future GOP Leader. In 1992, partially as a result of the House Bank controversy, he too declined to seek reelection. For Newt Gingrich to succeed as Bob Michel's heir, he will need to follow Cheney's cue in reaching out to various House Republican factions.

House Democrats. As Clausewitz wrote: "In war, the will is directed at an animate object that *reacts*."[66] When the minority is planning strategy against the majority, it must always remember that the majority may seize the initiative or respond in unpredictable ways. In the 1980s, House Democrats were blessed with leaders who skillfully manipulated Rubik's Cube against the GOP. Tip O'Neill and Claude Pepper used the Social Security issue to brilliant advantage, particularly in the 1982 election. Tony Coelho brought big business into the Democratic tent, and kept PACs from funding Republican challengers.

For a moment in 1989, House Republicans saw electoral profit in the ethics problems of Coelho and Jim Wright. Their timely resignations robbed the GOP of an issue and cleared the way for Speaker Foley and Majority Leader Gephardt. A GOP leadership aide said that the new Democratic team was every bit as partisan as the old, only more subtle about it. "They're reverse Chicken McNuggets: tender on the outside, crisp on the inside."

The Executive Branch. During the Reagan and Bush years, institutional imperatives often divided House Republicans from the White House. Moreover, the characteristics of the presidents and their advisers tended to widen the gulf. According to one Reagan official:

> In politics, the enterprise is larger than the star, and we failed to institutionalize the popularity of the star, to stretch it beyond him to the party and beyond his tenure in office. His core managers, the California group and First Lady, always concentrated on making the star popular.[67]

In the second Reagan administration, chief of staff Donald Regan further strained Hill relations with his haughty attitude. On February 21, 1986, he went to the Capitol Hill Club for a "fence-mending" meeting with House Republicans. When one member complained that the White House was not returning House GOP phone calls, Regan wagged his finger and shouted back: "I'm sick of that line! It's not true!" (One of the authors witnessed this exchange.) This conversation failed to generate warm feelings.

In the Bush administration, chief of staff John Sununu also had a prickly personality and a poor relationship with House Republicans. Richard Darman, the budget director, waged bureaucratic battles against White House aides who were trying to work with House Republicans on innovative policy ideas.[68] The only major figure in the Bush circle who cared much about winning House seats was Lee Atwater, the Republican national chairman. In early 1990, a brain tumor disabled Atwater. In his absence, the Republican National Committee drifted from its "command focus" on winning congressional seats in 1990.

Rubik's Cube and the Case of Taxes

The mention of the 1990 budget agreement calls to mind the issue of taxation. Starting in the late 1970s, most Republicans agreed that the core of a GOP appeal consisted of opposition to tax increases. Republicans who want limited government consider low taxes central to fighting the welfare state's growth. GOP strategists knew that the tax issue alone would not sweep their party to a House majority, but they considered it necessary to progress.

Although GOP tax attacks may have wounded Walter Mondale and Michael Dukakis in presidential campaigns, House Democrats hardly suffered a nick. In general elections between 1982 and 1990, Republicans beat just twenty-three incumbent House Democrats. According to election reviews in *Congressional Quarterly Almanac* and *The Almanac of American Politics*, most of these GOP pickups stemmed from redistricting, demographic changes, or local issues. In only about eight of those races were taxes apparently decisive, and Democrats eventually recaptured four of those seats.[69]

To make dramatic gains on the tax issue, all elements of the party would have had to unite against any tax increase. At every turn, Republicans would have had to maneuver House Democrats into defending higher taxes. During the 1990 budget debate, many Republicans looked wistfully back, thinking that they had taken such a course throughout the 1980s. Their memory tricked them. Even on this issue—the one subject that all Republicans supposedly agreed upon—they repeatedly failed. An examination of this failure demonstrates the workings of the political Rubik's Cube.

1980: The Squares Almost Line Up

In the months before the 1980 election, the Republicans seemed on the verge of solving their puzzle.

- **Interests.** In the late 1970s, inflation hurt taxpayers in two ways. Higher nominal home values meant higher property taxes. Higher nominal incomes pushed people into higher tax brackets even when their actual purchasing power stagnated. The result: a popular tax revolt, which started with California's Proposition 13 in 1978.[70] Meanwhile, business interests were also rebelling not only against higher taxes but intrusive federal regulation. Between 1970 and 1980, the annual number of pages in the *Federal Register* more than quadrupled.[71]

- **Institutions.** Democrats became the natural scapegoat for tax troubles, as they controlled the White House, both chambers of Congress, and the great majority of governorships and state legislative seats. Within the House of Representatives, procedures still enabled Republicans to make law and score political points. In 1978, for instance, William Steiger (R-Wisconsin) won passage of a landmark amendment to cut the tax rate on capital gains. And the GOP could still hope to oust a number of Democrats, since the incumbency advantage was not yet as daunting as it would become during the 1980s.

- **Ideas**. New Deal liberalism seemed obsolete while conservatism seemed refreshed. Foremost among the new conservative ideas was "supply-side economics," the proposition that tax cuts would encourage work, savings, and investment.[72]

- **Individuals**. In 1980, Ronald Reagan worked more closely with House Republicans than he would as president. Jack Kemp, Newt Gingrich, and David Stockman supplied him with advice and encouraged him to run with Republican congressional candidates as a team. Reagan had long championed tax cuts, and his House GOP allies stoked his antitax ardor. Meanwhile, at the Republican National Committee, Bill Brock was rebuilding the party's organizational base and renewing its intellectual vigor. He too knew the value of the tax issue.

With such a favorable alignment of the blocks, Republicans won a net gain of thirty-four seats. A majority appeared within their grasp—but Rubik's Cube was still turning.

Early Reagan Years

Institutional conflicts surfaced as early as 1981, with President Reagan's original tax-cut plan. To achieve a legislative success, and not merely to create an issue for the 1982 midterm, he needed Democratic votes. Throughout the debate, he downplayed partisanship and reportedly promised that he would not campaign against southern Democrats who backed his program. The deal irked some House Republicans, such as Daniel B. Crane of Illinois:

> If I were Reagan, I wouldn't have a thing to do with those guys. You look at their districts, those ought to be Republican seats. I would say they can go ahead, vote with Tip [O'Neill], and then we'll go into every one of their districts in '82 and say: "Elect a Republican because this guy blocked the president's program." And we'll have a majority in the next Congress."[73]

Forty-eight House Democrats voted for the Reagan tax cut.[74] Democrats who voted against it gained "cover" by supporting an alternative tax-cut plan by Ways and Means Chairman Dan Rostenkowski (D-Illinois). Both groups would fare well in the 1982 election.

Meanwhile, the economy started to slump and the deficit started to grow. A number of Senate Republicans were willing to consider a tax increase, but the House Republicans balked. David Stockman recalled White House contacts with party leaders: "The internecine warfare over taxes and the budget had become so severe that House and Senate Republicans were invited to separate meetings."[75] Stockman, James Baker, and Richard Darman eventually sold President Reagan on higher taxes. And with his support, the Senate passed the largest peacetime tax increase in history: $99 billion over three years. Republicans backed the tax increase 49-3; Democrats opposed it 1-44.[76]

The Reagan White House warned that the president would refuse to raise campaign money for House Republicans who voted against the tax hike. While his staff was threatening the House GOP, President Reagan was stroking House Democrats. To ease their fears that the Republicans would use the issue against them, Reagan promised personal thank-you letters to Democrats who voted for the bill. To complete the irony, the Republican National Committee—which had helped develop the party's antitax message in 1980—now committed $400,000 for advertisements supporting the tax increase.[77] Said Gingrich: "The fact is, on this particular bill, the President is trying to score a touchdown for liberalism, for the liberal welfare state, for big government, for the Internal Revenue Service, for multinational corporations, and for the various forces that consistently voted against this President."[78]

President Reagan did score his "touchdown." The conference report passed the House 226-207: R 103-89; D 123-118.[79] Later in the year, Congress also passed a nickel-a-gallon increase in the gasoline tax. Although it undercut their antitax rhetoric, a majority of House Republicans voted for it because various interests in their constituencies favored the projects it would finance. President Reagan signed it because his advisers thought he needed a "jobs bill" to fight the recession.

No Recovery on Taxes

In 1984, the economy was recovering, but the deficit remained high, so the president sought another deficit-reduction package. Although he said that he would not accept higher taxes until more spending curbs were in place, he signed a bill containing $50 billion in tax increases but only $13 billion in spending cuts. Republican senators backed the plan by a vote of 45 to 9, while a majority of House Republicans (76-86), voted against it.[80]

The split between Republican senators and House members showed up again that summer during debates on the party platform. Jack Kemp wanted a no-new-tax pledge without any reservations, while Bob Dole wanted to give the president some flexibility. Kemp's side won the platform battle. Reagan concentrated on his own reelection, however, refusing to use the tax issue against congressional Democrats.

In 1985, he revisited the tax issue from a different angle. This time, he proposed a "revenue neutral" tax reform that would reduce rates and make up the lost revenue by closing loopholes. Republican National Committee Chairman Frank Fahrenkopf said that tax reform could "assist in continuing [the] realignment." He added that the issue was associated with the Republican Party but "Democrats in the House will do everything they can to undercut that."[81]

Republicans faced several obstacles in making tax reform a ticket to electoral victory. First, many of the ideas behind reform sprang from Democrats such as Senator Bill Bradley, so both parties could plausibly claim "ownership" of the issue. Second, the prospect of losing tax preferences prompted interest groups to step up their campaign contributions to incumbents, particularly Democrats on the Ways and Means Committee. Third, institutional imperatives demanded bipartisanship. Reagan wanted a legislative achievement, not just a hot issue for the 1986 midterms. To pass a bill, he had to work with Chairman Rostenkowski, who in turn rebuffed House Republican efforts to participate in drafting the legislation. Fourth, personality problems hindered House GOP efforts on taxation: among other things, the ranking Republican on Ways and Means was past his prime and out of his depth.

When the bill came to the House floor, Republicans backed a successful effort to block consideration. President Reagan quickly won a reversal of the vote and preserved his reputation as a strong leader. But the split with the president left the House Republicans demoralized. Once again, Republicans had failed to speak with one voice on taxation.

And for all the struggle over the tax bill's passage, it proved a political bust. Americans simply did not believe that it improved the tax code. In a 1986 CBS/*New York Times* poll, only about a quarter of respondents said it would most benefit people like themselves.[82] After the bill's implementation, a *USA Today*/CNN poll found huge majorities calling the reform "complicated," "confusing," and "unfair."[83]

Following the 1987 stock-market plunge, President Reagan agreed to a budget summit that ended up proposing another tax increase. This time, Republicans in both chambers opposed the bill, though House Republicans did so by a much wider margin. The bill had sufficient Democratic support to pass, however, and President Reagan reluctantly signed it. The spirits of House Republicans sank further. On "Black Thursday," Speaker Wright had used a sharp procedural maneuver to pass an earlier version of the bill, and they had been powerless to stop him. Looking back over the previous few years, Gingrich said:

> By 1987 we have suffered by having failed to win decisively. We have suffered because we have been unable to make our case clearly, we have been unable to confront the left directly, and we have been unable to communicate with the vast majority which believes in our values but is confused by our own behavior.[83]

One need not agree with Gingrich's assessment of public values to conclude that Republicans had gained little ground from the tax issue. Institutional pressures had cracked the party's united front. Various tax increases had undermined the argument that the GOP was serving people's economic interests. The idea of "supply-side economics" was sounding stale to many Americans. And Republican leaders were pointing fingers at one another.

The Agony of the GOP 1990

Within a couple of years, however, many Republicans were again counting on the tax issue. They believed that George Bush's "no new taxes" pledge had won him the White House, and that the tax issue "belonged" to the GOP. House Republicans started 1990 with hope of avoiding the usual midterm seat loss. President Bush enjoyed record-high approval ratings, Republicans had matched Democrats in party identification for the first time in decades, and the economy was growing, albeit slowly. Ed Rollins, co-chairman of the National Republican Congressional Committee, said in March: "This is the best midterm election environment that we've had, at least in my lifetime as a Republican."[84]

But the Republicans could hope for extraordinary achievements only if their usual friction did not set in. And the friction took little time to arrive. GOP candidates across the country had been trying to score against their Democratic rivals by taking no-tax-increase pledges similar to Bush's. In May, the president hindered such tactics when he announced that he was agreeing to a budget summit with "no preconditions"—in other words, he would consider tax increases.

Republican hopes crashed with the president's June statement that a budget agreement should include "tax revenue increases." His reversal prompted scalding headlines ("READ MY LIPS—I LIED") and possibly doomed his reelection. Not wanting to get dragged down with him, House Republicans passed a resolution opposing any tax hikes. Mickey Edwards, chairman of the House Republican Policy Committee, said: "We admire the President, we support the President, but we don't work for the President."[85]

In mid-August, President Bush tried to satisfy Republican hardliners by criticizing congressional Democrats for overspending. His statement backfired because it clashed with his role as commander-in-chief. In response to the Persian Gulf crisis, he had just launched the largest military mobilization since Vietnam, and had called for bipartisan support. After taking political blows for this inconsistency, President Bush generally refrained from Democrat-bashing until the closing days of the 1990 campaign.

During the summit, President Bush had to compromise with House Democrats because of their overwhelming strength in the chamber. Summit participant Senator Phil Gramm (R-Texas) observed that this strength forced the president "to compromise much further than House Republicans have any desire of going. That's what produces the friction. . . ."[86] The summit produced an agreement with significant tax increases, which sparked opposition from most leading House Republicans. (Senate Republicans generally supported it.) Representative Steve Gunderson (R-Wisconsin), GOP deputy whip, explained: "We're up in 1990, and he's not. We're operating on a two-year cycle and don't want a recession this fall. He's looking at the bigger picture."[87]

Early on October 5, a majority of House Republicans voted against the summit agreement. Unwilling to pass the agreement without GOP support, Democrats also turned against it, and the agreement went down. House Democrats then passed a package more to their liking. House Republicans tried to shoot it down by offering their own alternative, but the majority ruled it out of order. Once again, the

House's majoritarian procedures worked against the political interests of the minority.

While the White House talked with congressional leaders to reach another budget deal, the GOP friction turned to fire. Ed Rollins of NRCC sent a memorandum to Republican House members and candidates:

> The President's approval/disapproval and job performance ratings have dropped precipitously. This is no doubt due to the lack of a budget resolution and the lack of a clear Republican position on taxes and spending. . . . Clearly, base Republican voters are confused about mixed signals coming from Republicans in Washington. They must be reassured about your positions. Understanding that several members have never taken a no tax pledge, my best advice today is to urge you to oppose taxes, specifically gas and income taxes. Do not hesitate to oppose either the President or proposals being advanced in Congress.[88]

The memo infuriated President Bush, who reportedly vowed not to sign any more NRCC fundraising letters while Rollins still worked there. But the financial damage to NRCC had already been done. "It's no secret that the shift on the tax position altered our fundraising dramatically," Rollins said later. "The first six months of last year were the best fundraising months we've ever had, the last six were the worst."[89]

Meanwhile, state politics added more to the fog of tax warfare. Republican Governor Bob Martinez of Florida suffered for his support in 1987 for a new tax on advertising, construction, and other services. He backtracked and won repeal of the tax, but allowed other tax increases. In Kansas and Nebraska, other GOP governors bled from Democratic attacks on their tax policies. In Illinois, Republican gubernatorial candidate Jim Edgar said he would try to persuade the state legislature to retain a 20 percent surcharge on state income taxes. Oddly enough, Edgar won.

At the federal level, Congress eventually passed a budget agreement, and GOP fears of massive losses proved to be exaggerated. Still, November belied the optimism of March. Republicans finished the 1990 elections with 167 seats, eight fewer than in 1988. GOP "spin doctors" claimed victory over the historical trend, noting that the in-party had lost an average of twenty-eight seats in midterms between 1946 and 1988. Such comparisons understated the damage to Republicans, however. As Rollins had noted the year before, no party holding the White House had ever entered a midterm with such a small share of House seats, so the loss of even a handful was bound to hurt.[90]

In 1992, the damage lingered. Despite redistricting and a large number of open seats, Republicans made only a modest gain in the House. In the Voter Research and Surveys exit poll, one-fifth of the respondents said that President Bush's tax reversal was very important to their presidential choice. Of these voters, more than three-fourths voted for Democratic House candidates.[91]

The Turn of the Cube?

Just as the 1980 election had generated euphoria among House Republicans, the weeks after the 1992 election were mired in melancholy. As Clausewitz wrote, a fighting spirit "will only grow in the soil of constant activity and exertion, warmed by the sun of victory."[92] In defeat, morale withers.

Springtime brought better news with signs that the Rubik's Cube of House Republican fortunes might be twisting again. Under unified government, Democrats had to take responsibility for the bad as well as the good. Republicans in both chambers were relieved of carrying White House water, and could now concentrate on playing offense. President Clinton gave them ammunition by failing to deliver the middle-class tax cut that he had promised. At the individual level, the new House Republicans proved a feisty lot, willing to take on partisan challenges. The 1993 budget battle climaxed in a one-vote victory margin, with all House Republicans opposed. The outcome was an opposition researcher's fondest hope: every Democrat who voted for the plan could be charged with casting the decisive vote for a huge tax increase. Republicans looked forward to translating the budget vote into 1994 midterm election upset victories over Democratic incumbents.

Later that year, however, disunity came back to haunt the House GOP. When John Kasich (R-Ohio) and Tim Penny (D-Minnesota) proposed $90 billion in additional spending cuts, several senior Republicans on the Appropriations Committee warned fellow Republicans that projects in their districts might die if they supported the cuts.[93] Eighteen Republicans voted against the proposal, which lost by six votes.

Autumn also found House Republicans working with the Clinton White House in passing the North American Free Trade Agreement, while Democrats defected in droves. Some Republicans hoped that

NAFTA marked the start of bipartisan cooperation. The political danger, however, was that future presidential overtures could divide or co-opt the House Republicans. By giving members of the minority a small voice in policymaking, the White House could dull their partisan edge.

It was too early to predict serious Republican gains. Democrats held onto their knack for courting interest groups, and were now claiming the title of "the party of new ideas." House Republicans worked hard to regain the title, with little success. "The public seems largely unaware that Republicans have produced alternative programs on deficit reduction, crime, immigration and campaign finance," wrote columnist Morton Kondracke at the end of 1993. Kondracke also noted that the House GOP had a serious health-care reform proposal, but "the only publicity the GOP has garnered came last week when it secured a Democratic National Committee memo suggesting that Democratic activists crowd last weekend's 57 GOP health care town meetings."[94] As Michel had warned several years before, the mainstream media give scant attention to Capitol Hill, frustrating House Republican attempts to win the battle of ideas.

The puzzle remained unsolved.

Notes

1. Gary C. Jacobson, *The Electoral Origins of Divided Government* (Boulder, Colo.: Westview Press, 1990); Morris P. Fiorina, *Congress: Keystone of the Washington Establishment*, 2d. ed. (New Haven: Yale University Press, 1989).

2. Alexis de Tocqueville, *Democracy in America*, trans. George Lawrence, ed. J. P. Mayer (Garden City, N.Y.: Doubleday/Anchor Books, 1969), 12.

3. Tocqueville, *Democracy in America*, 287.

4. Tocqueville, *Democracy in America*, 305.

5. Pendleton E. Herring, *Group Representation Before Congress* (Baltimore: Johns Hopkins University Press, 1929), 47.

6. James W. Ceaser, *Reforming the Reforms: A Critical Analysis of the Presidential Selection Process* (Cambridge, Mass.: Ballinger, 1982), 157–63.

7. In *Congressional Politics*, Christopher J. Deering uses three levels of analysis: individual, institutional and environmental. If the definition of "environment" includes interests and ideas, then our model has much in common with Deering's. Christopher J. Deering, *Congressional Politics* (Chicago: Dorsey, 1989), 3.

8. *The Federalist*, ed. Jacob E. Cooke (1961; reprint, Middletown, Conn.: Wesleyan University Press, 1982), number 10, p. 59.

9. Tocqueville, *Democracy in America*, 57; *The Federalist*, number 10, p. 59.

10. U.S. Council of Economic Advisers, *Economic Report of the President* (Washington, D.C.: U.S. Government Printing Office, 1993), 380, 396.

11. Jacobson, *The Electoral Origins of Divided Government*, 112–20.

12. Michael Barone, *Our Country: The Shaping of America from Roosevelt to Reagan* (New York: Free Press, 1990), 202.

13. U.S. Department of Commerce, *Statistical Abstract of the United States 1993* (Washington, D.C.: U.S. Government Printing Office, 1993), 18.

14. Ibid., 787.

15. Ibid., 436.

16. For data on the largest PACs, see Larry Makinson, *The Cash Constituents of Congress* (Washington, D.C.: CQ Press, 1992), 24.

17. Quoted in Brooks Jackson, *Honest Graft: Big Money and the American Political Process* (New York: Alfred A. Knopf, 1988), 69.

18. Alan Ehrenhalt, *The United States of Ambition* (New York: Times-Mirror/Random House, 1991), 125–42.

19. Ronald M. Peters, Jr., *The American Speakership: The Office in Historical Perspective* (Baltimore: Johns Hopkins University Press, 1990), 283.

20. Quoted in Brian Lamb, *C-SPAN: America's Town Hall* (Washington, D.C.: Acropolis, 1988), 120.

21. Deering, *Congressional Politics*, 5.

22. Michael J. Malbin, "Factions and Incentives in Congress," *Public Interest* 86 (Winter 1987): 100.

23. *The Federalist*, number 10, p. 57.

24. *The Federalist*, number 50, p. 346.

25. See Richard Hofstadter, *The Idea of a Party System* (Berkeley: University of California Press, 1969), 53; James MacGregor Burns, *The Deadlock of Democracy: Four-Party Politics in America* (Englewood Cliffs, N.J.: Prentice Hall, 1963), ch. 1.

26. *The Federalist*, number 10, p. 64.

27. Woodrow Wilson, *Congressional Government* (Cleveland: Meridian, 1956 [1885]), 210.

28. Carl Von Clausewitz, *On War*, ed. and trans. Michael Howard and Peter Peret (Princeton: Princeton University Press, 1984), 357.

29. Ibid., 119.

30. Thomas E. Mann, "Is the House of Representatives Unresponsive to Political Change?" in *Elections American Style*, ed. A. James Reichley (Washington, D.C.: Brookings, 1987), 276–78.

31. Quoted in Tim Curran, "Ed Rollins Looks Back on Two Tumultuous and Disappointing Years as Head of NRCC," *Roll Call*, February 7, 1991, 8.

32. Linda L. Fowler and Robert D. McClure, *Political Ambition: Who Decides to Run for Congress* (New Haven: Yale University Press, 1989), 195–98.

33. Sidney M. Milkis, *The President and the Parties: The Transformation of the American Party System Since the New Deal* (New York: Oxford University Press, 1993), 274.

34. Deering, *Congressional Politics*, 9.

35. Herring, *Group Representation Before Congress*, 48.

36. Quoted in Thomas B. Edsall, "GOP: Ideological Divide," *Washington Post*, July 14, 1990, A6.

37. Quoted in John M. Barry, *The Ambition and the Power* (New York: Viking, 1989), 304.

38. Bill Whalen, "Party Animal," *Campaigns and Elections*, November 1990, 32.

39. Quoted in David Broder, "At White House Order," *Washington Post*, January 23, 1991, A17.

40. Quoted in Lee Byrd, "House GOP Leader Unthrilled by Reagan Landslide," Associated Press, November 8, 1984.

41. *The Federalist*, number 51, p. 350.

42. Barbara Sinclair, *Majority Leadership in the U.S. House* (Baltimore: Johns Hopkins University Press, 1983), 112-114.

43. Quoted in Helen Dewar, "Republicans Wage Verbal Civil War," *Washington Post*, November 19, 1984, A5.

44. Quoted in David Shribman and David Rogers, "Relationship is Tense Between Republicans in House and Senate," *Wall Street Journal*, May 1, 1985, 22.

45. Ibid., 22.

46. Ibid., 1.

47. Quoted in Milkis, *The President and the Parties*, 269.

48. *The Federalist*, number 57, p. 386.

49. James W. Ceaser, *Liberal Democracy and Political Science* (Baltimore: Johns Hopkins University Press, 1990), 201.

50. Morris P. Fiorina, *Congress: Keystone of the Washington Establishment*, 2d. ed. (New Haven: Yale University Press, 1989), ch. 5.

51. Linda K. Kowalcky, "Congressional Staff Organization and Re-Election Strategies in the U.S. House of Representatives" (paper presented at the annual meeting of the Southern Political Science Association, Atlanta, November 5-7, 1992).

52. Robert Michel, Remarks at the National Press Club Awards for Consumer Journalism, Washington, D.C., December 6, 1989.

53. Ibid.

54. Norman Ornstein and Michael Robinson, "The Case of Our Disappearing Congress," *TV Guide*, January 11, 1986, 4-10; Timothy E. Cook, *Making Laws and Making News: Media Strategies in the US House of Representatives* (Washington, D.C.: Brookings, 1989), 58-59.

55. *The Federalist*, number 1, p. 3.

56. George F. Will, *Restoration: Congress, Term Limits and the Recovery of Deliberative Democracy* (New York: Free Press, 1992), 98.

57. Phil Duncan, "Looking Beyond Gridlock," *Congressional Quarterly Weekly Report*, January 16, 1993 supplement, 11.

58. Gary C. Jacobson, "Congress: Unusual Year, Unusual Election," in *The Elections of 1992*, ed. Michael Nelson (Washington, D.C.: CQ Press, 1993), 172.

59. William G. Mayer, *The Changing American Mind: How and Why Public Opinion Changed Between 1960 and 1988* (Ann Arbor: University of Michigan Press, 1992), ch. 6.

60. Ibid., 456.

61. Kevin Phillips, *The Politics of Rich and Poor* (New York: Random House, 1990). For a skeptical view of Phillips's argument, see James Q. Wilson, "Malaise II," *Commentary*, October 1990, 54–56.

62. Quoted in Paul Taylor, "For GOP and Nominee, A Fight to Hold Ground," *Washington Post*, August 14, 1988, A1.

63. Ibid.

64. E. J. Dionne, *Why Americans Hate Politics* (New York: Simon and Schuster, 1991), 318–19.

65. Patrick J. Buchanan, "Crackup of the Conservatives," *Washington Times*, May 1, 1991, G1.

66. Clausewitz, *On War*, 149.

67. Quoted in Paul Taylor, "For GOP and Nominee, A Fight to Hold Ground," *Washington Post*, August 14, 1988, A1.

68. Charles Kolb, *White House Daze: The Unmaking of Domestic Policy in the Bush Years* (New York: Free Press, 1994), 202–3.

69. All eight of these Democratic defeats occurred in 1984: McNulty (Arizona); Patterson (California); Andrews, Britt, and Clarke (North Carolina); Hightower, Patman, and Vandergriff (Texas). The Andrews, Clarke, Hightower, and Patman seats eventually went back to the Democrats.

70. Thomas Byrne Edsall and Mary D. Edsall, *Chain Reaction: The Impact of Race, Rights and Taxes on American Politics* (New York: W. W. Norton, 1991), ch. 6.

71. Harold W. Stanley and Richard G. Niemi, *Vital Statistics on American Politics* (Washington, D.C.: CQ Press, 1992), 271.

72. Former Reagan advisor Martin Anderson says that, contrary to myth, Reagan never claimed that a reduction in tax rates would pay for itself. Martin Anderson, *Revolution* (New York: Harcourt, Brace Jovanovich, 1988) 153–57.

73. Quoted in Margot Hornblower and T. R. Reid, "After Two Decades, the 'Boll Weevils' Are Back and Whistling Dixie," *Washington Post*, April 26, 1981, A10.

74. *Congressional Quarterly Weekly Report*, August 1, 1981, 1375.

75. David Stockman, *The Triumph of Politics* (New York: Avon, 1987), 380.

76. *Congressional Quarterly Weekly Report*, July 31, 1982, 1855.

77. *Congressional Quarterly Weekly Report*, August 21, 1982, 2035.

78. *Congressional Record* (bound), 97th Congress, 2d sess., August 17, 1982, 21416.

79. *Congressional Quarterly Weekly Report*, August 21, 1982, 2100.

80. *Congressional Quarterly Weekly Report*, June 30, 1984, 1578–80.

81. Quoted in Peter M. Gianotti, "Tax Plan: Battle for Credit," *Newsday*, July 5, 1985, 13–17.

82. CBS press release, October 6, 1986.

83. Mindy Fetterman, Poll: New Tax Law is Unfair," *USA Today*, April 14, 1988, B1.

84. *Congressional Record*, daily ed., November 30, 1987, H10735.

85. Ed Rollins, "Politics in the 1990s," address to the Association of Homebuilders Legislative Conference, Washington, D.C., March 5, 1990.

86. John E. Yang and Tom Kenworthy, "House GOP Takes Stand Against Any Tax Increase," *Washington Post*, July 19, 1990, A7.

87. Bill Whalen, "For Republicans, A House Divided," *Insight*, November 12, 1990, 10.

88. Rollins memo reprinted in *Washington Post*, October 25, 1990, A21.

89. Tim Curran, "GOP Congressional Campaign Committees Are Deeper in Debt Than Democratic Counterparts," *Roll Call*, February 11, 1991, 3.

90. Ed Rollins, address to luncheon meeting of Women in Government Relations, Washington, D.C., August 9, 1989.

91. VRS press release, November 3, 1992.

92. Clausewitz, *On War*, 189.

93. Major Garrett, "GOP Rift Develops in House; Some Help Clinton Fight Spending Cuts," *Washington Times*, November 22, 1993, A1.

94. Morton M. Kondracke, "GOP Rivals Clinton In New Ideas Dept., But Nobody Knows," *Roll Call*, December 6, 1993, 6.

Chapter 6

Novembers of Discontent

Republicans finished the 1992 elections with just 176 House seats, a slight gain from 1990, but short of the figure that the GOP had anticipated a year before, and well below the 192-seat "glass ceiling" that the party had touched three times in recent decades. Some Republicans blamed President Bush for dragging down the party with the lowest share of the popular vote of any president since William Howard Taft in 1912. Although a better showing by Bush might have helped the GOP, one can hardly credit the congressional results to Clinton's five-point margin. Of the 258 districts won by Democratic House candidates, Clinton scored a higher percentage than the winner in only *four*.[1]

This chapter analyzes the party's performance in congressional elections, showing the impact both of structural influences (redistricting and incumbency) and political ones (the GOP's narrow electoral base). These related problems defy quick solutions.

Redistricting

When asked to account for their party's failure to win a majority, House Republicans usually cite gerrymandering, the drawing of congressional district boundaries so as to give unfair advantages to a political party; in this case, the Democrats. And when challenged to back up their complaint, they point to the gap between their share of House seats and their share of the total popular vote in House elections. With fair district lines, they argue, the former would equal the latter, and the GOP would have more seats.

As political scientists have often explained, this line of reasoning

Figure 6-1
Republican Seats and Votes in House Elections
1946–92

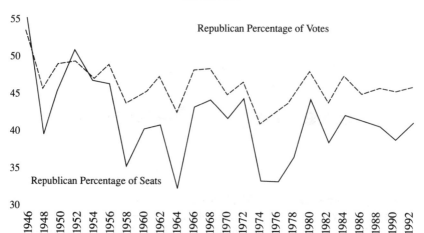

Source: Norman J. Ornstein, Thomas E. Mann, and Michael J. Malbin, *Vital Statistics on Congress 1993–1994* (Washington, D.C.: CQ Press, 1994), 49–50.

has several shortcomings.[2] First, the total GOP House vote last topped the Democratic vote in 1952, and last broke 50 percent in 1946. Even if the share of seats perfectly matched the share of votes, Democrats would still have enjoyed the longest stretch of majority status in history.

Second, a seat-vote gap need not imply unfair districts. In any winner-take-all electoral system, the party with the most votes will tend to get a disproportionate share of seats. Consider a hypothetical system with three fairly drawn districts of equal size. If party A gets 51 percent in two districts while party B gets 52 percent in the third, party B will get 50 percent of the total vote but party B will win only 33 percent of the seats. A real-world example comes from the 1992 contests for New Mexico's three seats, which ended with one Democratic landslide, one Republican landslide, and one modest Republican victory. Though Republican House candidates barely won 50 percent of the vote statewide, they got 67 percent of the seats—under district lines drawn by Democrats. For the nation, the difference between the GOP's share of votes and House seats averaged 6.2 percent between 1972 and 1980. Although Republicans complained of unfair redistricting after the 1980 census, the average seat-vote gap *shrank* to 5.2

percent between 1982 and 1990. In 1992, with new district lines, the gap was 5.1 percent.

Third, the seat-vote gap also reflects turnout differences in the parties' constituencies. Congressional apportionment hinges on the total number of residents instead of the number of voters. The first figure comprises not only voters but eligible adults who abstain from registering and voting, and people who cannot lawfully vote because of age or alien status.[3] Many Democratic lawmakers come from areas where poverty and poor education discourage potential voters. A number of Democratic districts also have large ethnic-minority populations, which include high numbers of minors and noncitizens. So although all districts in a state must have equal *populations*, Democratic districts often have smaller *electorates*: of the thirty districts where turnout fell below 150,000 votes in 1992, Democrats won in twenty-nine.[4] Republicans tend to represent affluent constituencies with higher turnout, so it usually takes more votes to elect a Republican than a Democrat.[5]

Fourth, even in states where Democratic gerrymanders have disappeared, Democratic House candidates have often continued to fare well. Throughout the 1980s, Republicans pointed to the California gerrymander, in which a Democratic governor and legislature had sought partisan advantage by sculpting congressional districts into outlandish shapes. In 1990, the Rorschach outline of one such district graced the cover of a Republican National Committee pamphlet on the evils of gerrymandering. After the census of that year, a Republican governor and Democratic legislature could not agree on new districts, so the California Supreme Court appointed special masters to draw the lines. Most observers said that the new districts treated the GOP fairly. What was the result? Before the 1992 election, the party held nineteen of California's forty-five seats, or 42 percent of the state delegation. If gerrymandering had constituted the GOP's main problem, this percentage should have risen under the new lines. It did not: after the 1992 election, the GOP had twenty-two of fifty-two California seats, still just 42 percent.

Just as Republicans err by exaggerating the impact of redistricting, political scientists sometimes err by dismissing it. The 1992 elections indicate that districts do make some difference. Although no California Democratic incumbent lost in the general election, some suffered greatly diminished margins in their new constituencies. In 1988, Richard Lehman of the San Joaquin Valley romped with 70 percent, and in

1990, he ran unopposed. In 1992, with a new district, he had to outspend his opponent six-to-one just to win a 1,029-vote squeaker.

During the 1990s redistricting, Republicans hoped to benefit from the 1982 Voting Rights Amendments, which apparently required map-makers to draw districts with heavy concentrations of minority groups. With these normally Democratic blocs "packed" into a small number of districts, reasoned GOP strategists, the surrounding constituencies might become more Republican. And the GOP also hoped that the new legal requirements would have the side effect of breaking up existing maps that had favored Democrats. In some cases, the election results justified these expectations. In Illinois, where new minority districts helped disrupt an extreme gerrymander, the Democratic advantage in congressional seats dropped from 15–7 to 12–8.[6] Minority districts had an even greater effect in Georgia, where the Democratic lead went from 9-1 to 7-4.

In several other instances, however, Democrats used their control of redistricting to meet legal requirements without sacrificing partisan interests. The North Carolina map, later the subject of court challenge, used bizarre shapes to protect Democrats while creating two new minority districts. Because of such maneuvers, the creation of new minority districts directly led to the defeat of only three Democratic incumbents: Ben Erdreich of Alabama, Tom McMillen of Maryland, and Jerry Huckaby of Louisiana.[7]

On June 28, 1993, the U.S. Supreme Court reopened the issue of racial gerrymandering when it reinstated the challenge to the North Carolina map, which a lower court had dismissed. This decision did not settle the question of whether the North Carolina districts were constitutional; rather, it merely held that the judiciary had to deal with the plaintiffs' argument that the gerrymander had deprived them of equal protection of the law. In effect, the Court invited further litigation on issue. And by now, the national GOP had changed course: recognizing that its minority-district strategy had largely failed, it filed an *amicus curiae* brief on behalf of the plaintiffs. Praising the Court's decision, the Republican National Committee's new chief counsel said that it "raises the question of [whether] the automatic creation [of majority-minority districts] is in the best interest of the democratic process."[8] Whether motivated by racial or partisan interests, gerry-mandering has probably shaped electoral politics in subtle and indirect ways. In a district that heavily favors one party, even the highest-quality challenger may expect to win, say, 40–45 percent of the vote. Under this circumstance, the good potential candidate forgoes the race, and the party either mounts no challenge at all or runs a poor candidate who gains only 30–35 percent. In the context of racial gerrymandering, Chandler Davidson refers to this phenomenon as "candidate diminution."[9] Although the number of "unseen candidates"[10] is hard to reckon, candidate diminution has sapped the GOP's talent pool and depressed the party's total share of the popular vote in House elections. If so, the seat-vote gap understates the importance of gerrymandering, because redistricting affects both seats *and* votes.

Again, because we are dealing with hypotheticals (who would have run under different lines), this point is speculative—yet the 1992 results are at least consistent with it. With new and somewhat more competitive districts, the GOP ran more candidates with elective experience than it had in recent elections[11] and it won its highest share of the total House vote since 1984.

Incumbency and "Perks"

The power of incumbency, Republicans believe, ranks just behind gerrymandering as a source of Democratic dominance. In recent decades, the reelection rate has seldom dipped below 90 percent; and because Democrats have more seats, it would stand to reason that their party gains more from incumbency than the GOP.

As with gerrymandering, incumbency does not work quite as simply as it may first seem. By definition, the incumbency advantage does not apply to races for open seats: those where the incumbent has died, retired, or lost the party nomination. Republican enthusiasts might expect that their party would be making gradual progress in open seats, since it would be playing on a more level field. Yet in open-seat contests between 1982 and 1992, the GOP's losses completely offset its gains. The GOP's failure to make long-term net gains among open seats has led some observers to conclude that the Republicans have no case, and that the incumbency advantage is largely irrelevant to party control of the House.

This conclusion goes too far in the other direction. In most recent elections, Republicans have had to defend a disproportionate share of open seats, because Republicans have chosen to leave the House more often than Democrats. Between 1980 and 1992, on average, each election year saw 9.8 percent of Republicans retire or seek other office, compared with 7.1 percent of House Democrats. Even in 1992, when redistricting, overdrafts, and early expectations of a weak Democratic ticket led 15.4 percent of Democratic incumbents to step down, the GOP rate lagged only slightly, at 14.4 percent.

A retirement robs a party of the incumbency advantage in the district and reduces the likelihood that it can hold the seat. According to Gilmour and Rothstein, House Republicans' tendency toward early retirement has cut GOP strength in the House by five to fifteen seats.[12] Why have House Republicans chosen to weaken their party by jumping ship? One likely explanation lies in minority status itself: with no hope of ever chairing a committee, and given the shrinking influence of ranking minority members, House Republicans find that other career options become more appealing. In 1987, minority whip Trent Lott looked longingly at the Senate, where Republicans had recently held a majority and could still score legislative victories. "Sure that attracts you—the attractiveness of winning more votes, of being in the majority. I like winning like anybody."[13] The next year, he successfully ran for the Senate, and a Democrat picked up his House seat. In 1990, the GOP lost several other seats when incumbents tried for the Senate.

In a 1992 interview, Republican Leader Michel singled out Fred Grandy (R-Iowa) "as one doing his homework and able to handle his own down there on the floor and mix it up with some tough assignments. It's made me feel good about giving him the plum on Ways and Means, because he's used it to good advantage." In 1993, Grandy announced that he was giving up his seat to run for governor.

Republicans who seek reelection do not make out quite as well as their Democratic colleagues. Between 1982 and 1990, forty-two seats held by Republican incumbents went to Democrats, compared with twenty-three Democratic seats that went the other way. The pattern seemed to reverse itself in 1992, when defeat visited sixteen Democratic incumbents and only eight Republicans; however, unusual circumstances account for this outcome. Of the losers, three Democrats and two Republicans faced other incumbents because of redistricting, so their defeats are not comparable to the others. Though redistricting did not pit Democrat Ben Erdreich of Alabama against another incumbent, it did replace his minority constituents with Republicans, so he went down. Four Democrats and one Republican had made at least 100 overdrafts at the House Bank. Two other Democrats labored under a cloud of criminality: Mavroules of Massachusetts had been indicted on corruption charges, and Bustamante of Texas was under investigation. (Both were later convicted.) Excluding these exceptional cases leaves six Democrats and five Republicans.

Among the incumbent winners of 1992, Democrats had an average of 65.4 percent of the vote, compared with 63.4 percent for Republicans. And 30.8 percent of winning Democratic incumbents had 70 percent of the vote or more, while only 23.6 percent of the Republicans scored as high.[14]

What accounts for these differences? One source of the incumbency advantage lies in lawmakers' access to valuable official resources, called perquisites or "perks." At public expense, they can send newsletters and other mail to their constituents, make frequent trips home, use sophisticated broadcasting facilities, and hire aides to solve constituent problems and bring more federal spending to their districts. These resources, which boost the political standing of incumbents, are worth at least $1.5 million per two-year House term.[15] Although the evidence here is sketchy at best, Democrats may be using these resources more shrewdly than Republicans. Democrats tend to allocate a greater share of their personal staffs to district offices, where the aides work more directly with constituents than in Washington offices.[16] Of the twenty-five House members who spent the most on franked mail during the first eight months of 1992, seventeen were Democrats.[17] Some of the top frankers (such as Tom Downey of New York) went down to defeat, but others (Les Aspin of Wisconsin and Nita Lowey of New York) won tough contests.

Political scientists disagree about the extent to which perks can influence elections, but House Republicans believe that perks give an edge to the majority party.

Campaign Finance

Campaign finance loomed as the great equalizer in 1980, when the average GOP challenger spent nearly as much as average Democratic incumbent. Then the "equalizer" turned against Republicans. Especially after 1984, GOP challengers fell far behind, and many of them could not even begin to compete. In 1992, they did better than in the past few elections; nevertheless, less than a third of Republican challengers could raise the $200,000 that most observers regard as the minimum for a competitive campaign. True, Democratic challengers also had fundraising difficulties, but their party did not have to defeat a single Republican incumbent to hold their majority.

The GOP's frustration fed on itself. The trivial seat pickup that accompanied the 1984 Reagan landslide drove home the point that the Republicans would not retake the House in the near future. This realization affected fundraising because many individuals and interest groups give campaign money in order to gain access to influential lawmakers. Backing GOP challengers was now a no-win proposition: if they lost, the contributions might antagonize powerful majority-party incumbents, and even if they won, they would never chair committees. Poor fundraising hurt GOP prospects, which in turn hurt fundraising.

Democratic leaders worked to accelerate this cycle. "Business has to deal with us whether they want to or not," said Tony Coelho (D-California), chair of the Democratic Congressional Campaign Committee (DCCC). "I tell them, 'You're going to have to work with us.' "[18] Just as important, Democrats have warned businesses against supporting GOP challengers. "We're going to be a majority for a very long time," said Coelho in 1986, "so it doesn't make good business sense to give to Republicans."[19] These unsubtle tactics have worked. While the GOP's incumbents continued to do well, its challengers and open-seat candidates were getting starved—even by corporate PACs, formerly a Republican cash cow. After 1986, Republicans got less than half of corporate PAC funds, mainly because of declining contributions to their non-incumbent candidates (Table 6-1).

Meanwhile, DCCC protected Democratic members. In 1990, the National Republican Congressional Committee (NRCC) targeted a number of seemingly vulnerable Democrats. As soon as PAC directors got the target list, recalls an NRCC official, they took it to DCCC,

Table 6-1
Republican Share of PAC Contributions to House Campaigns
1978–92

	All PACs			Corporate PACs		
	Incumbent	Challenger	Open Seat	Incumbent	Challenger	Open Seat
1978	19%	12%	10%	28%	16%	12%
1980	24	15	7	32	20	9
1982	30	7	7	45	9	9
1984	26	8	4	39	11	6
1986	29	3	6	42	3	7
1988	28	2	4	42	3	4
1990	26	2	5	38	3	6
1992	24	3	6	34	4	7

Source: Federal Election Commission; and Ornstein, Mann, and Malbin, *Vital Statistics on Congress 1994*, 102–5.

which then made sure that the listed incumbents got all the PAC money they needed. In Michigan's 11th Congressional District, this tactic allowed David Bonior to outspend his challenger by more than three to one. And NRCC's problems did not stop there.

The Party Bureaucracy: Nightmare on First Street

In the late 1970s and early 1980s, the National Republican Congressional Committee and the Republican National Committee supplied unprecedented levels of support to candidates, and aired broad party messages to national audiences. From their headquarters on First Street, S.E., Republican operatives dreamed that their own know-how would at last restore their party to majority status.

By the time of the Bush administration, these dreams seemed naive. After the party's disappointment in the wake of the 1990 budget deal, a startling admission came from Ed Rollins, outgoing co-chair of NRCC:

> The day of the national committees being a significant force in American politics is over. We've spent a decade now in which the three buildings— the one I work in [NRCC], the one next door [Republican National Committee] and the Senate committee—have raised and spent over a billion dollars. That may have kept us somewhat in a minority status or it may have protected us from further annihilation. I can't say which.[20]

It is tempting to disregard Rollins's remark as the frustrated outcry of a man embittered by his party's performance and by his own conflicts with the Bush administration. Yet in our interviews with Republican lawmakers and others in the GOP political community, we found great dissatisfaction with NRCC.

- A House Republican who feuded with Guy Vander Jagt called NRCC a "rotten operation" that "spends money on consultants rather than on candidates."

- A onetime Republican leadership staffer said that "NRCC frittered away enormous resources during the 1980s because they never had a warrior at NRCC."

- A member of the GOP leadership said: "We're not learning. The RNC and NRCC continue to blast Congress expecting the public to distinguish between Democrats and Republicans. They've sent fundraising letters attacking Congress into Republican members' districts!''

- Said a western lawmaker who later went down to defeat: "The NRCC is out of touch, though we should give credit where credit is due: they've done a superb job providing technical advice for redistricting. But besides that, I don't know what they do over there."

- Said an NRCC staffer: "We should blow the place up."

Some assessments have been more favorable. Following his 1989 special-election victory, Craig Thomas of Wyoming wrote: "The entire NRCC staff served me and my campaign with professional assistance and advice. As in any effort, there were early organizational problems, but overall the work of the NRCC was proficient and on target."[21] But note that even this comment was stilted and hedged. Moreover, it was the exception to the rule.

Why does NRCC get so little respect? Why has it had so little success? In a candid interview, Guy Vander Jagt stressed structural limitations, including the House GOP's frustration with a legislative agenda shaped by the other party. "Frequently, when we have a vote on the floor, members will say to me, 'Guy, send a mailing on this vote to key districts.' But we've never really found a tremendously successful formula for doing that. The connection is not that direct." Similarly, the organization can do little to affect the economy or presidential popularity. "We at the NRCC cannot create the climate or the national trends. We're a burp in a wind storm."

Many observers nonetheless think that NRCC could have done a better job, and their most frequent criticisms concern the organization's spending. Under federal law, a party committee may give each House candidate up to $5,000 per primary, runoff, and general election. On behalf of individual candidates, a party committee may also spend additional sums, called "coordinated expenditures," for such things as district-level polls and advertisements. According to critics, NRCC has wasted contributions and coordinated expenditures on losing campaigns, and shortchanged promising candidates such as Will Scott of Kentucky, who lost his 1990 challenge to incumbent Carl C. Perkins by only two percentage points.[22] Three of six successful GOP challengers of 1990—Scott Klug (Wisconsin), Rick Santorum (Pennsylvania), and Frank Riggs (California)—got the back of NRCC's hand until their victory celebrations. "They kept telling me my polls were no good," said Santorum. "They had a real inside-the-Beltway mentality: unless you use our people, we don't believe anything you say."[23] "How much help did I get?" he asked rhetorically. "None. Not a penny. Not necessarily a kind ear."[24]

The NRCC is responsible to GOP House members, and critics argue that incumbents have benefited at the expense of challengers and open-seat candidates. As one NRCC aide said: "We have a serious problem with all those pigs at the trough." As for contributions and coordinated expenditures, such criticisms fall wide of the mark: careful studies have shown that only a small fraction has gone to safe incumbents.[25] During the 1990 cycle, NRCC suspended automatic contributions to incumbents—many of whom got angry and supported Don Sundquist's challenge to Guy Vander Jagt's chairmanship.[26]

But data on contributions and coordinated expenditures tell only part of the story. In recent campaign seasons, such direct assistance has accounted for less than one-fifth of NRCC outlays (Table 6-2). During the 1990 cycle, NRCC outspent its Democratic counterpart by 277 percent, yet gave its candidates only 14 percent more in direct help. In the next cycle, co-chair Spencer Abraham and executive director Tom Cole sought to streamline the operation and slash spending on consultants. Yet a large disparity persisted: while outspending DCCC by 170 percent, it gave only 18 percent more in direct assistance.

Table 6-2
Finances of the National Republican Congressional Committee and the Democratic Congressional Campaign Committee

	Total Spending		Direct Assistance (and as % of spending)	
	NRCC	DCCC	NRCC	DCCC
1983–84	61.7	0.2	8.8 (14%)	1.9 (19%)
1985–86	40.8	12.6	5.8 (14%)	2.2 (17%)
1987–88	33.7	12.5	5.7 (17%)	3.1 (25%)
1989–90	34.4	9.1	3.8 (11%)	3.3 (36%)
1991–92	34.3	12.7	5.9 (18%)	5.0 (39%)

Figures in millions of dollars. Direct assistance figures are the sum of contributions and coordinated expenditures. Source: Federal Election Commission.

In 1990, an NRCC spokesman defended the allocation pattern, noting that the committee had carefully studied races where it had spent the legal maximum in direct aid: "We found out it didn't have a huge impact."[28] Other supporters of NRCC say that much of the "overhead" has gone to toward worthy activities such as absentee-ballot programs and generic party advertising. Critics respond that NRCC has failed to make a systematic appraisal of the political value of overhead activities.

In part, this dispute reflects the national-strategy vs. local-strategy debate, for the generic party ads were an attempt to draw national attention to party themes. By the early 1990s, most House Republicans agreed that the party needed a mix of local and national themes, but there was little consensus on the contents of such a mix. In any case, "party nationalization" turned out to be more a sentiment than a coherent strategy, for NRCC never stuck to a long-range plan for gaining seats. Moreover, it sent out mixed messages. On the one hand, NRCC tried to make a national issue out of the official advantages enjoyed by Democratic incumbents; on the other hand, it published *Incumbent!*, a newsletter that advised GOP lawmakers on how to use those advantages themselves.

Overhead spending entails opportunity costs as well as direct costs. That is, every dollar going to First Street is a dollar unavailable to candidates and party organizations at the grass roots. In the course of financing the party bureaucracy, NRCC and its sister committees drained much of the GOP donor pool by excessive reliance on direct-mail appeals.[28] Some donors "tapped out" and many potential donors stopped opening fundraising mail after receiving dozens of over-wrought appeals to save the world from Tip O'Neill. The upshot: Republican candidates at all levels found it increasingly difficult to raise their own funds.

During the 1982 cycle, NRCC plied PACs with rosy assessments of party prospects; and when the GOP lost ground, PAC directors felt betrayed.[29] In 1990, it made candidates meet stiff bureaucratic require-ments (e.g., presentation of poll results) to receive party aid. As a result, Vander Jagt forthrightly remembered, "many candidates were so busy trying to jump through our hoops that they forgot about their own campaigns."

Notwithstanding praise for aides such as redistricting chief Thomas Hofeller, many have blamed the staff, which runs NRCC's day-to-day operations. In 1989, *National Review* urged House Republicans to "dump the expensive and incompetent NRCC Washington bureaucracy.''[30] A Republican operative specializing in southern politics dismissed the NRCC staff as "second and third tier people short on experience and talent, who have an inside-the-Beltway mentality, and who do not connect with real people." A House Republican leadership aide recalled arriving in Rochester only to be greeted by "an NRCC kid" who knew the way to the hotel but "knew absolutely nothing about Rochester." An NRCC aide called the organization's field division "a group of guys in blue blazers under thirty who think they're all Roger Ailes. . . . They all brag about how many states they're going to fly into in the next five days. They don't get it: campaigns don't want our people. Campaigns want money and research."

Asked about the Beltway yuppie mentality, a 27-year-old NRCC aide replied: "We're not just a bunch of stiffs in Brooks Brothers suits—well, actually, I guess all I own *are* Brooks Brothers suits—but we're not all just concerned about where the next cocktail party is. There are a bunch of us who are seriously concerned about the future of our country, the direction of our inner cities, racial problems."[31]

A former high-ranking NRCC official thinks that the organization fell prey to the cult of political expertise:

We've overprofessionalized the system: we've tried so hard to make an industry and science out of campaigning that we've lost creativity and imagination. We have paint-by-number campaigns. We wrongly assumed that if you did a technically good campaign, you'd win, that if you did the technical stuff right, a strategy would emerge.

In his 1990 post-mortem, Ed Rollins contrasted the GOP's public policy with its party organization:

We have become a party that is exactly contrary to what our philosophy is. Our philosophy has always been to decentralize things and push them back to where the people are. As a party, we have tried to centralize everything and bring everybody here to Washington.[32]

In the 1992 cycle, Abraham and Cole acted in accord with those observations and tried to decentralize NRCC. Both got high grades, especially for their recruiting efforts. But while applauding the duo, one top staffer warned:

It is a superficial analysis to suggest that just because Spence Abraham and Tom Cole are from outside Washington, that NRCC has solved its problems. Yes, there is a little different perspective at NRCC today. But there is no *revolution*. Our tenure is too short. We have to focus on the 1992 race. Therefore, any changes are at the margins.

Combined with a decade's worth of internal troubles, the hostile political climate of 1992 brought bad times to NRCC, and the committee ended the cycle nearly $8 million in debt. New NRCC chairman Bill Paxon (R-New York) reacted by cutting the NRCC staff by three-fourths and persuading more than a hundred GOP lawmakers to pledge that théy would give or raise money for the committee. Nevertheless, the debt remained heavy, prompting rumors that NRCC was considering bankruptcy protection. Meanwhile, DCCC held a splashy press conference to announce that its fundraising had improved so much that it had retired its debt. The NRCC executive director explained that "We lost the White House" and have not been "shaking down every interest group" as the Democrats had.[33]

Amid the ongoing turmoil at the committee, some Republicans remembered the disquieting words of Mickey Edwards: "I've been saying for years that Democrats have been winning elections in the House because they don't have an NRCC."[34]

Split Tickets and Grass Roots

The Republican Party's problems extend from First Street to Main Street. In recent decades, the party's weakness at the grass roots has prevented it from turning strength at the presidential level (at least through 1988) into winning campaigns for lower offices. If Republicans candidates had won every House district that George Bush carried in 1988, they would have taken a House majority by better than a two-to-one margin. Instead, Democratic candidates won nearly half of the districts that went to Bush (Table 6-3).

These figures may exaggerate the GOP presidential base, because many districts went to Bush by slim margins. While Bush carried 68 percent of congressional districts, he won only 54 percent of the two-party popular vote. But Republicans could still have won a *226-seat* majority if they had only won those districts where Bush got 55 percent or better. Another way of underscoring the partisan imbalance is to look at each presidential candidate's strongest districts: Democrats took ten of Bush's top fifty districts, while only one of Dukakis's top fifty went to a Republican: William Green of New York. And the GOP later had trouble keeping the thirteen Dukakis districts that it had won

Table 6-3
Winners of 1988 House and Presidential Races in
Congressional Districts

		Districts carried by	
		Bush	Dukakis
Districts won by	Republican House Candidate	162	13
	Democratic House Candidate	135	125

Calculated from: Rhodes Cook, "Key to Survival for Democrats Lies in Split-Ticket Voting," *Congressional Quarterly Weekly Report,* July 8, 1989, 1710.

in 1988. By 1992, five had gone to Democrats (including Green's) and one had been eliminated by reapportionment.

A comparison of the 1992 presidential and congressional vote yields a murkier picture because Ross Perot apparently hurt Bush in normally Republican districts. The extent of the GOP's difficulty becomes clearer when we look at its performance by region (Table 6-4). Since the 1960s, the South and the West have been the GOP's most consistent

Table 6-4
Republican Share of House Seats by Region

	Total Number of Seats Per Region		Percentage of Total Held by Republicans					
	1980 Census	1990 Census	1982	1984	1986	1988	1990	1992
Northeast	95	88	39%	43%	42%	42%	40%	42%
Midwest	113	105	45%	45%	45%	43%	40%	42%
South	142	149	27%	35%	32%	33%	33%	38%
West	85	93	45%	48%	47%	47%	44%	41%

As before, we follow the census definition of geographical regions. *Northeast:* Maine, New Hampshire, Vermont, Massachusetts, Connecticut, Rhode Island, New York, New Jersey, Pennsylvania. *Midwest:* North Dakota, South Dakota, Nebraska, Kansas, Minnesota, Iowa, Missouri, Wisconsin, Illinois, Michigan, Indiana, Ohio. *South:* Texas, Oklahoma, Arkansas, Louisiana, Kentucky, Tennessee, Mississippi, Alabama, West Virginia, Virginia, Maryland, Delaware, North Carolina, South Carolina, Georgia, Florida. *West:* Alaska, Hawaii, Washington, Oregon, California, Idaho, Nevada, Utah, Arizona, Montana, Wyoming, Colorado, New Mexico, source of electoral votes. In 1980, Reagan carried every western state except Hawaii and every southern state except West Virginia, Maryland, and Carter's home state of Georgia. The House Republicans took heart not only from Reagan's showing but from the forthcoming shift of House seats to the Sunbelt. They figured that they could build upon their already-significant numbers in the West and finally make their long-awaited breakthrough in the South. But the desired gains never materialized. In the 1982 elections, Democrats took ten of the seventeen new seats in the South and West.[35]

Ten years later, the GOP did gain ten seats in the South. As mentioned earlier, three GOP victories came as the direct result of minority districts in Alabama, Louisiana, and Maryland, and three more stemmed from the Georgia remap. Still, the results fell short of Republicans hopes. Mississippi's five-member delegation remained all-Democratic even though three of the seats had been in Republican hands at one point or another during the 1980s. The GOP could not even topple Jamie Whitten, who had been weakened by illness and the impending loss of his chairmanship of the Appropriations Committee.

In the West, the GOP never won half the seats even during Reagan's heyday, and the party finished the 1992 election with a net gain of only one seat. Consider Utah—arguably the GOP's most reliable state—where Democrats won two of three seats in 1992. In the Second District, Republicans thought they might have a chance when incumbent Democrat Wayne Owens gave up his seat to run for the Senate. Yet even without the incumbency advantage, Democrat Karen Shepherd kept the district in her party's column. Granted, the Second District has a concentration of Democrats in Salt Lake City; but consider the Third District, a small-town Mormon constituency that had given 69 percent of its vote to George Bush in 1988 and 77 percent to Reagan in 1984. In 1990, Democratic candidate Bill Orton won there with 58 percent. Although his GOP candidate had shortcomings, the 1990 result was no fluke: two years later, Orton won reelection with 59 percent.[36] In short, Democrats could often take Republican seats, but Republicans could seldom take Democratic seats. Before delving further into causes and cures, we must look at two other dimensions of the GOP's problem: its weakness among minority voters and its inability to win urban districts.

The Minority Vote and the Minority Party

Although Republican presidential candidates have failed to win much support from blacks and Latinos, they have more than compensated among whites.[37] Except for the 1964 Johnson landslide, the GOP carried the white vote in *every* presidential election between 1952 and 1992.

Compared with their party's presidential contenders, Republican House candidates have not done as well with white voters, while doing just as poorly among blacks and Latinos (Table 6-5). Despite the House GOP's sporadic efforts to woo ethnic minorities, most have continued to see the Republican Party as the party of the white businessman and the opponent of civil rights.[38]

A 1989 memorandum prepared for national Republican leaders described the results of black focus groups:

> Blacks perceive the Republican Party as the party of the rich. To them, our main policy goal is to preserve the economic status quo which leaves them out. In no way do they see us as the party of economic opportunity and advancement for everyone. This basic belief about us undermines the credibility of several of the arguments we thought should help us with blacks.

During the Reagan years, black alienation from the GOP deepened as a result of the proposal to grant tax-exempt status to segregated schools; the President's initial opposition to the Martin Luther King holiday; and the 1986 GOP "ballot security" program, an apparent effort to strike blacks from voter rolls. Bush did not create as much personal resentment, but his "minority outreach" suffered from controversy over civil rights legislation and the political emergence of

Table 6-5
Ethnic Groups and GOP House Vote

Percent of two-party vote for Republican House candidates

	1982	1984	1986	1988	1990	1992
White	46%	54%	51%	50%	50%	50%
Black	11%	8%	14%	15%	21%	11%
Latino	25%	31%	25%	24%	28%	28%

Source: CBS and VRS exit polls in Harold Stanley and Richard G. Niemi, *Vital Statistics on American Politics*, 4th ed. (Washington, D.C.: CQ Press, 1994), 109–10; VRS news release, general election, November 3, 1992. The 1990 GOP uptick among blacks may have resulted both from random error and faulty sampling.

David Duke. In 1993, the GOP's reputation among black voters suffered another blow. Ed Rollins, who ran the successful campaign of the party's candidate for governor of New Jersey, claimed after the election that his side had made cash payments to discourage turnout drives in black neighborhoods.

Racial voting has hurt the GOP in congressional elections. In districts with many minority voters, Republicans have lost whenever Democrats have mobilized their minority base and won just a modest fraction of the white vote. At the same time, however, Republicans have not been able to count even on the "whitest" districts in the land. In 1988, Republicans won only half of the constituencies where the black population was 10 percent or less; and beyond that point, the greater the black population, the greater the Democratic share of seats.[39]

Among the most heavily black and Latino constituencies, Republicans have been effectively locked out. In 1984, a white Republican edged a black Democrat in a race for the black-majority Second District of Mississippi. White and blacks were highly polarized, and the Republican had more success in turning out his supporters. In 1986, black Democrat Mike Espy took the seat by mobilizing blacks and neutralizing hostility from whites. (Before his selection as Agriculture Secretary, Espy made further progress among his rural white constituents by appearing in advertisements for the National Rifle Association.)

Redistricting after the 1990 census produced a record number of majority-minority districts. In 1992, Democrats won all thirty-two black-majority districts and sixteen of twenty Latino-majority districts. Of the four GOP victories in the latter category, two came from Florida's Cuban districts, which are atypical because Cubans are far more likely to vote Republican than are other Latinos. In Texas, Latino Republican Henry Bonilla did defeat incumbent Democrat Albert Bustamante, but only after the latter came under an ethics cloud. And in California, Robert Dornan held onto the 46th District mainly because many of the Latinos in the constituency are not yet citizens and so cannot vote.

These results cast further doubt on the GOP strategy of deliberately encouraging the construction of majority-minority districts. Unless Republicans can win a greater share of the minority vote, these districts will constitute an electoral fortress for the Democrats, without providing a comparable fortress for the GOP. According to a Republican operative:

The GOP has great potential in the South because of the existing vacuum, but the politics of race dooms you to nail-biting elections. For example, in South Carolina if you only get 5 percent of the black vote, you need 68 percent of the white vote. . . . Any Republican candidate must start by asking: Can I get any black votes?

Before redistricting gave him a largely white constituency, Thomas Bliley of Virginia was one of the rare Republicans who appeared able to win black votes. Blacks made up 28 percent of the district's voting-age population, but between 1982 and 1990, Bliley's vote never dipped below 59 percent. Bliley even carried the majority-black city of Richmond. He stayed away from polarizing issues, instead supporting aid to historically black colleges and sanctions against South Africa. In an interview, Bliley drew lessons for his party:

Most Republicans abandoned the black vote, which was not very smart politically. An important rule in politics is never concede anything to your opponent, even if only to force him to protect his base. Besides, we need to represent *all* constituents. We should look at it as a long-term investment, even if we have little success with some groups during the first or second election.

Town and Country

Republican House candidates used to have a fighting chance in the cities. Places such as the Bronx, Queens, Newark, San Francisco, Chicago, and Milwaukee all used to have at least some Republican House members. And in 1946, Republicans carried all six districts in Philadelphia.[40] Since then, however, urban America has become a Republican desert. After the 1990 census, there were eighty-seven House districts with a majority of their people living in central cities.[41] In 1992, Republicans won fourteen. Of these, ten were in Sunbelt cities such as Phoenix or Lubbock, and only four were in the Northeast and Midwest: Christopher Shays (R-Connecticut), Susan Molinari (R-New York), John Kasich (R-Ohio), and Deborah Pryce (R-Ohio).

The presence of large minority populations helps explain GOP fortunes. The Republican Party scarcely exists in most urban black or Latino neighborhoods, where winning the Democratic primary is tantamount to election. GOP candidates have also had difficulty in city districts without a sizable minority presence.

One might assume that Republicans make up for their urban disadvantage by winning in the countryside. In fact, however, most rural House members have been Democrats. As we have just seen, Republicans have failed to make a breakout in the South, which accounts for a disproportionate share of rural constituencies. In 1992, there were thirty-four southern districts with majority-rural populations, and only six elected Republicans. The GOP won twenty-two of the thirty-six non-southern rural districts; even so, the Democrats managed to capture thirteen of these seats. (One went to Socialist Bernard Sanders of Vermont.) A particularly galling defeat came when COS member Vin Weber (R-Minnesota) was replaced by liberal Democrat David Minge.

Republicans do better in the suburbs. In 1992, there were 191 districts where a majority of the population lived in metropolitan areas outside the central cities. Republicans won 102 of these districts, or 53 percent of the total. But this lead is hardly overwhelming, and it does not come close to compensating for the Democrats' advantages elsewhere. While Republicans can seldom win in cities, Democrats have fielded attractive candidates who can consistently win Republican-leaning suburbs. New York's First District, at the eastern end of Long Island, gave 66 percent of its vote to Reagan in 1984 and 60 percent to Bush in 1988. Yet in 1986, Democrat George Hochbrueckner won an open-seat race to succeed Republican-Conservative William Carney. Like other suburban Democrats, Hochbrueckner has survived through careful attention to constituent service and local concerns such as the Grumman Corporation, where he used to work.

Finally, there were eighty-seven districts with various mixes of rural, urban, and suburban areas. In 1992, Democrats took fifty-five and Republicans won thirty-two.

Demography, Destiny, and Strategy

Gazing upon all the gloom of the preceding pages, a Republican might seek solace in an overarching trend: growing Republican party identification among young voters. Although the change has yet to show up in aggregate voting data, the argument goes, the new Republican generation will soon increase GOP representation across the board. Polling data fail to support such a prediction: between 1982 and 1992, younger voters were no more likely to support GOP House candidates than were their elders.[42] The young may be identifying with the Republican Party, but they have little brand loyalty.

The analogy is useful: in congressional politics, as in consumer economics, markets have become segmented. Democrats have thrived precisely because they have supplied different kinds of candidates to different kinds of constituencies. They have dominated certain segments of the political market, and held their own in others. Through the 1980s, Republicans acted like Detroit auto makers: they kept peddling the same old models, so they were shut out of many segments of the market, and started to lose their grip on the rest.

Furthermore, they were starting to see competition from an unexpected source: minor parties. It is still hard to gauge the impact of third parties in congressional elections, in part because the news media often do not report on their performance. But fragmentary evidence suggests that they have influence. In 1992, minor-party candidates received 6.9 percent of the congressional vote in California; and in nine of the state's House races, they won a percentage that equaled or exceeded the winner's margin.[43] Although some minor-party candidates have diverted votes from the Democrats, the growing strength of these candidacies may pose a threat to the GOP, particularly if they appeal to the "outsider" sentiment that Republicans want to tap. According to a poll for *U.S. News and World Report*, an independent candidate backed by Ross Perot's organization could pull up to 11 percent from a Republican in a generic House race.[44]

To attain a majority, Republicans do need to regain their hold on their traditional constituencies. But they probably cannot amass such a lead among white, affluent, suburban districts that they can ignore the rest. Battles are won through conquest, not just consolidation. A Republican strategy must include an "invasion" of Democratic territory, an effort to win more districts where poor people and minorities have a significant presence. This effort can be entirely consistent with Republican principle: HUD Secretary Jack Kemp showed it is possible to apply conservative ideas to the problems of non-Republican constituencies. Representative Thomas Bliley provides a less famous but equally useful model. He has articulately described how federal policies should help families and encourage personal responsibility. And as a former mayor and small businessman, he has also been a good listener: he knows the issues that matter to his constituents, both black and white.

Republicans could gain seats by attacking the twin evils of gerrymandering and incumbency, but solving these structural problems will not take them all the way to a majority. They need to address their own weaknesses, both at the level of national organization and at the grass roots. They must examine the political markets and assess the problems with their own electoral base.

Notes

1. Richard E. Cohen, "What Coattails?" *National Journal*, May 19, 1993, 1285–91.

2. Norman J. Ornstein, "The Permanent Democratic Congress," *The Public Interest* 100 (Summer 1990): 24–44.

3. Howard A. Scarrow, "One Voter: One Vote: The Apportionment of Congressional Seats Reconsidered," *Polity* 22 (Winter 1989): 253–68.

4. Rhodes Cook, "House Republicans Scored a Quiet Victory in '92," *Congressional Quarterly Weekly Report*, April 17, 1993, 967.

5. James E. Campbell, "Divided Government, Partisan Bias and Turnout in Congressional Elections: Do Democrats Sit in the 'Cheap Seats'?" (paper presented at the annual conference of the American Political Science Association, Washington, D.C., August 29–September 1, 1991).

6. Colleen McGuiness, ed., *CQ's Guide to 1990 Congressional Redistricting*, Part I. (Washington, D.C.: CQ Press, 1993), 27–50.

7. Bob Benenson, "GOP's Dreams of a Comeback Via the New Map Dissolve." *Congressional Quarterly Weekly Report*, November 7, 1992, 3580–81.

8. Quoted in Dave Kaplan, "Constitutional Doubt Is Thrown On Bizarre-Shaped Districts," *Congressional Quarterly Weekly Report*, July 3, 1993, 1761.

9. Chandler Davidson, "Minority Vote Dilution: An Overview," in *Minority Vote Dilution*, ed. Chandler Davidson (Washington, D.C.: Howard University Press, 1989), 3.

10. The phrase *unseen candidates* comes from Linda L. Fowler and Robert D. McClure, *Political Ambition: Who Decides to Run for Congress* (New Haven: Yale University Press, 1989), 3.

11. Gary C. Jacobson, "Congress: Unusual Year, Unusual Election," in *The Elections of 1992*, ed. Michael Nelson (Washington, D.C.: CQ Press, 1993), 167–70.

12. John B. Gilmour and Paul Rothstein, "Early Republican Retirement: A Cause of Democratic Dominance in the House of Representatives," *Legislative Studies Quarterly* 18 (August, 1993): 345–65.

13. Quoted in Jeffrey Birnbaum, "House Republicans, Frustrated in Minority Role, Often Ask Themselves Whether It's Time to Leave," *Wall Street Journal*, June 5, 1987, 52.

14. Ryan M. Iwasaka, "The Power of Incumbency in the 1992 Election" (unpublished manuscript, Claremont McKenna College, Claremont, California, 1992).

15. Gary C. Jacobson, *The Politics of Congressional Elections*, 3d ed. (New York: HarperCollins, 1992), 38.

16. Mark Zupan, "Why Congress Is the Democrats' Game," *Wall Street Journal*, October 20, 1989, A14.

17. Glenn R. Simpson, "Surprise! Top Frankers Also Have the Stiffest Challenges," *Roll Call*, October 22, 1992, 1, 15.

18. Robert Kuttner, "Ass Backward: A Bestiary of Democratic Money Men," *New Republic*, April 22, 1985, 21.

19. Paul Houston, "Democrats Relying More on Special-Interest Funds," *Los Angeles Times*, October 30, 1986, I-1.

20. Ed Rollins, "The Future of the Republican Party," address to the Republican Communication Association, Washington, D.C., December 14, 1990 (authors' transcription from C-SPAN broadcast).

21. Letter, *National Review*, November 10, 1989, 6.

22. Chuck Alston, "Those Who Needed It Least Often Got Campaign Help," *Congressional Quarterly Weekly Report*, December 29, 1990, 4236; Mike Pieper, "Red Tape Strangles Challengers," *Campaign*, February 1991, 1, 7.

23. Quoted in Janet Hook, "The Political Advice of Rick Santorum," *Congressional Quarterly Weekly Report*, April 6, 1991, 886.

24. Quoted in Jackie Calmes, "GOP Turns Upon Itself Over Financial Charges Involving Party Congressional Committee's Staff," *Wall Street Journal*, November 30, 1990, A16.

25. Paul S. Herrnson, "Party Strategy and Campaign Activities in the 1992 Congressional Elections" (paper presented at the conference on "The State of the Parties: 1992 and Beyond," Ray C. Bliss Institute, Akron Ohio, September 23–24, 1993); Diana Dwyre, "Is Winning Everything? Party Strategies for the U.S. House of Representatives" (paper presented at the annual meeting of the American Political Science Association, Chicago, September 3–6, 1992).

26. Robin Kolodny, "Congressional Party Politics and the Congressional Campaign Committees: The 1990 Leadership Challenge to Rep. Guy Vander Jagt" (paper presented at the annual meeting of the American Political Science Association, Washington, D.C., August 29–September 1, 1991).

27. Quoted in Alston, "Those Who Needed It Least," 4237.

28. Tim Hames, "The Changing Shape of Republican Party Finance in the 1980s" (paper presented at the annual meeting of the American Political Science Association, San Francisco, August 30–September 2, 1990).

29. Brooks Jackson, *Honest Graft: Big Money and the American Political Process* (New York: Alfred A. Knopf, 1988), 77.

30. Wick Allison, "How to Win an Election," *National Review*, October 13, 1989, 24.

31. Quoted in "Young in GOP Find a Cruel World," *New York Times*, August 18, 1993, A8.

32. Rollins, "The Future of the Republican Party."

33. Quoted in Tim Curran, "A First! DCCC Is Free of Debt," *Roll Call*, December 6, 1993, 13.

34. Quoted in Donald Lambro, "House GOP Chiefs Weigh War Plans," *Washington Times*, March 15, 1991, A12.

35. Rob Gurwitt, "Redistricting Bitter Disappointment to GOP," *Congressional Quarterly Weekly Report*, November 6, 1982, 2787.

36. Michael Barone and Grant Ujifusa, *The Almanac of American Politics 1994* (Washington, D.C.: National Journal, 1993), 1290–91.

37. Thomas Byrne Edsall and Mary D. Edsall, *Chain Reaction: The Impact of Race, Rights, and Taxes on American Politics*, (New York: W. W. Norton, 1991); Peter Brown, *Minority Party: Why Democrats Face Defeat in 1992 and Beyond* (Washington, D.C.: Regnery Gateway, 1991). We do not include Asians and Pacific Islanders in our analysis because they constitute a much smaller share of the population than blacks or Latinos. There are only twenty-four districts where they account for more than 10 percent of the voting-age population, and only two (both in Hawaii) where they have a majority.

38. Stuart Rothenberg and Charles Cook, "Most Blacks Will Remain Democrats," *Wall Street Journal*, January 24, 1986, 24.

39. Bernard Grofman, Robert Griffin, and Amihai Glazer, "The Effect of Black Population on Electing Democrats and Liberals to the House of Representatives,"*Legislative Studies Quarterly* 17 (August 1992): 368.

40. David R. Mayhew, *Party Loyalty Among Congressmen* (Cambridge, Mass.: Harvard University Press, 1966), 71.

41. Authors' calculations from U.S. Department of Commerce, Bureau of the Census, *Population and Housing Profile: Congressional Districts of the 103d Congress* (Washington, D.C.: Government Printing Office, 1993).

42. See exit poll data in Harold W. Stanley and Richard G. Niemi, *Vital Statistics on American Politics*, 4th ed. (Washington, D.C.: CQ Press, 1994), 109; and VRS news release, general election, November 3, 1992.

43. Ryan M. Iwasaka, "Minor Party Candidates in California Congressional Elections" (unpublished manuscript, Claremont McKenna College, Claremont, California, 1993).

44. Gloria Borger and Jerry Buckley, "A Giant New Sucking Sound," *U.S. News and World Report*, December 20, 1993, 20.

Chapter 7

Remedies

As we have argued throughout this book, House Republicans are fragmented by interests, institutions, individuals, and ideas. Like any legislative party, the House GOP is split along regional, generational, and economic lines. These fractures are compounded by institutional structures including the separation of powers, federalism, and bicameralism. Individual ambitions and political ideas also divide the Republicans. These differences of opinion include quarrels over how to win the majority.

When we asked what House Republicans could do about their predicament, members and staff offered four basic views. First, some fatalists saw the party's status as beyond the House GOP's control. Among other things, they cited voter preference for congressional Democrats, majority party abuse of House procedures, partisan gerrymandering, and GOP weakness in the states. Second, advocates of the "national" solution proposed to turn House elections into referenda on broad national issues. Third, supporters of the "local" approach wanted to emphasize community concerns to win seats one by one. Fourth, some simply called on their GOP colleagues to stop attacking one another; such infighting, they insisted, accounts for much of the party's minority dilemma.

In this chapter, we argue against both fatalism and bickering. Solving a Rubik's Cube is difficult, yet possible. Bickering does hurt the House GOP, but internal peace would not be enough to win a majority. The second and third views make more sense, and can complement each other. A party needs broad national issues to attract good candidates and build voter identification, and it needs grass-roots strength to translate generic support into concrete victories. By themselves, House Republicans can neither define national issues nor build their party at the local level. They need the support and cooperation of Republicans from the presidency to the precinct. As we have seen, that help can be hard to come by.

We start this final chapter by asking whether individual House Republicans care enough to address their party's dilemma, and whether it makes sense for them to try. Next we consider the merits of the "national" and "local" schools in the words of their proponents and critics. Finally, we return to our Rubik's Cube analysis to appraise ways of balancing these approaches.

Desperately Seeking Majority?

In the summer of 1992, when we asked a former top leadership aide whether House Republicans were really hungry for a majority, he shouted: "No! They don't care any more than the American people care about the budget deficit!" A retired ranking member amplified this point:

> House Republicans would like to be a majority, sort of. Some are comfortable, for example the appropriators, highwaymen, and senior bulls. Some are confrontational toward fellow Republicans. All work, in the last analysis, to save their own asses first, last, and always. It's a busy life; other people's campaigns are not their first priority.

In this view, the comfortable are complacent, the confrontational consume their own, and all are concerned with reelection. Oddly, this member would not fit into his own categories.

A former party leader elaborated on the difference between the comfortable and the confrontational.

> I think you need to make distinctions and in some respects the most important criterion by which you can distinguish House Republicans is whether they are really committed to this notion of building a majority or whether they're primarily in it to perpetuate their own positions. And so to some extent, that gets back to this debate that rages between those who say all politics is local and those who want a national campaign strategy. There . . . has been a growing desire to be part of the majority. There were people who you would classify ordinarily as moderate Republicans who get along with Democrats who were all of a sudden bomb-throwers, folks who voted for Newt Gingrich for whip.

When we asked another leader, who lost his bid for reelection, to identify the fault lines in the House GOP, he said:

I would divide it into those who feel their first and last job is to elect a Republican majority, those who are reaching out, lashing out and forcing votes [and] those who on the campaign trail bash the Democrats but the rest of the week are serious legislators. For example, Bob Michel wanted to work out economic growth legislation with Rostenkowski. Newt and Bob Walker were looking for wedge issues.

Both former leaders agreed that the mix of comfortable and confrontational members has changed. They cited a growing desire for a majority, with some "moderate, reasonable Republicans" suddenly becoming "bombthrowers" willing to put Newt Gingrich in the leadership. This transformation stems in part from deliberate efforts to change members' preferences. According to Gingrich:

There's no question that when I first came here the majority of the caucus preferred passively accepting Democratic dominance and fighting them within a framework which the Democrats and the establishment created. . . . [But the freshman] class of 1978 took on as one of their conscious projects the reestablishment of Republican identity and Republican morale.

Gingrich, perhaps the House Republican most intensely committed to majority status, held onto his zeal despite near-defeats in 1990 and 1992. If reelection were his main goal, he was not behaving as a "rational actor"; yet as Richard Fenno notes, lawmakers are complex creatures who care about other things.[1] Gingrich, like a growing number of Republicans, is willing to divert some of his political capital from the pursuit of reelection to the pursuit of party power.

The frustrations of minority status are pushing more Republicans into confrontationism, and Gingrich believes that he now has a "critical mass" in support of his efforts. The House Republicans' attitude may puzzle political scientists as much as it does House Democrats. But as Dick Cheney explained after the McIntyre-McCloskey fight:

It may be the Democrats don't understand the depth of feeling because they've never served in the minority. They get the good committee assignments. If you've got a good idea on a bill, chances are it will end up with a Democrat's name on it. We don't control the floor. The only thing we control is Special Orders.[2]

To those who care about power and policy—and not just reelection—such frustrations sharpen their appetite for majority status. Most House Republicans acknowledge that they have only limited power to satisfy this drive. One recently retired moderate concluded: "If Republicans are to be a majority, that majority can't be built from the inside." House Republicans can provide a foundation for a majority, he argued, but their efforts will necessarily be "feeble": recall Guy Vander Jagt's description of NRCC as "a burp in a windstorm." Even party activists acknowledge that the House GOP is working at the margins. In 1992, the ever-optimistic Gingrich saw "80 percent of the problem" as beyond his colleagues' reach. That year's election altered the House GOP's calculations by reducing its legislative power while at the same time increasing its political flexibility.

During a GOP administration, Republicans in both the House and Senate have at least some relevance for policy negotiations when they can hold onto the one-third-plus-one vote necessary to sustain a veto. Even without the White House, the Senate Republicans are still formidable when they can muster the forty-one votes needed to block cloture. In the House, by contrast, a Democratic presidency practically eliminates any residual leverage for a badly outnumbered GOP. Except in rare instances where the Democrats are severely split (e.g., the North American Free Trade Agreement), Republicans may as well forget about legislating and play to the galleries, looking to build an eventual majority.[3] Bush's defeat thus enhanced Gingrich's position.

It also gave House Republicans more control over their fate and more leeway to divest themselves of responsibility for legislating. Although Gingrich regretted the election of Bill Clinton, he said that it represented the House GOP's "liberation from the tentacles" of the Bush administration: "We are a party that is more risk-taking in doing new things."[4] During both the Reagan and Bush administrations, the desire to support the White House worked against the desire to fight the Democrats: the McIntyre-McCloskey conflict fizzled out when House Republicans saw that further disruptions would hamper the administration's program. Under a Democratic administration, they could now let the other side worry about the consequences for the executive branch.

One measure of House Republicans' increased commitment to majority status might be a willingness to reorganize themselves. At the start of the 103d Congress, Michel appointed a task force to study reform of the dispersed leadership structure. One proposal would eliminate the five elective leadership posts below the level of Conference Chair, replacing them with an executive council. At the same time, leadership aides began drafting a "takeover plan" pointing out the practical consequences if the party does gain control. The plan reportedly identified one challenge as reversing the growth of congressional staffs, presumably at the committee level.[5]

All That Jazz

We turn again to the national and local strategies. The nationalizers often lash out at ranking members, since the committee system competes with the party and constituents for members' loyalty. One COS member claimed that "ranking members tend to be more liberal and more inclined to go along to get along." He disliked "the tendency of committee ranking members to protect their turf." The inclination of committee ranking members to "go along to get along" thwarts the House Republicans' ability to sharpen partisan lines, thereby undercutting the national strategy.

The localizers do not just listen in silence to these charges. Retired GOP moderate Barber Conable was sharply critical of the COS wing: "The infighting within the GOP is counterproductive. They look like caterwauling kids, immature and strident. I don't like stridency. I don't like game playing; it's more important to try to influence policy." House Republican infighting, according to Conable, is one key reason they remain mired in the minority. "You stand in the corner and posture, and you become demoralized and irresponsible and irrelevant. The Democrats as a permanent majority become arrogant and flabby. Neither feels the need to compromise."

Conable questioned the tendency to think "everything is subsumed under the great fight to become the majority." He added: "Gingrich is into game playing, posturing over in the corner. He enjoys the battle for its own sake. . . . Newt thinks everybody is hanging on his words." Conable echoed House Republicans who see Gingrich's approach as more symbolic than substantive.

A key party aide observed, "I used to sit in sessions at NRCC where Newt would posit his latest theory . . . he's so good at theorizing, and yet there's never any follow through." A top staff ally of the "responsible partners" faction maintained, "The COS people always talk 'big concepts,' but never provide, or work, on any details. The [1992] economic growth package is a good example." He went on to say, "Strategically they're very naive . . . You must know the substance of an issue before you can successfully strategize." This leading GOP committee aide concluded that the Gingrich wing of the party is "anti-committee," and inclined to see others as "captives of the committee system."

The localizers can also articulate their own perspective. According to a top leadership staffer: "The NRCC must be very pragmatic. It can't be ideological. It must develop profiles of districts and match them with profiles of possible candidates." In an implicit criticism of the confrontational wing, this person insisted: "The key is *organization* not *media* politics. We've got to get back to building local organizations. We've got to be willing to ask someone to vote, to ask someone to raise money." A long-time Republican committee staff director added that the flaw of the national strategy is that "congressional elections involve decisions about an individual rather than a policy." Hence, all politics is not ideological, as Barber Conable emphasized:

> Any party that plays too much with ideology is risking its existence. The problem with ideology is that it excludes people. Parties have constituencies rather than ideologies, and the constituency of the Republican Party is the middle class. . . . The House Republicans are flirting with ideology today. . . . The party needs to go back to the basics, and quit eating our young. I am against litmus tests that produce clones incapable of compromise.

For their part, the nationalizers warn that excessive pragmatism can drag the party into brain-dead blandness. If the party becomes too fearful of excluding anyone, they argue, it grows incapable of exciting anyone. For them, ideas count. They bitterly remember the political consequences of the Bush years, when arrogant policy brahmins such as Richard Darman sneered at the "vision thing" and Beltway professionals dismissed their concerns as "mere ideology." The nationalizers recognize that American politics is open to the energy of new ideas, and they are optimistic about change. They have a natural feel for the dynamism of our political system, seeing beyond the friction of institutional politics to the potential "fission" of partisan realignments. Indeed, the nationalizers regard themselves as policy entrepreneurs trying to spark what Gingrich calls the "necessary revolution."

An analytical shortcoming of the national strategy, however, is that it underestimates the connections among ideas, institutions, and interests. It is hard to foster party government in a fragmented constitutional system and a society that embraces an increasingly diverse array of groups and philosophies. Many of the nationalizers are perceptive about a decentralized and participatory society, but sometimes seem to argue for a centralized message and strict discipline. Said an all-politics-is-local critic of Gingrich:

> Newt and I get along pretty well; he's added energy to the Conference. But with Reagan, we had a chance to win a majority, and instead we focused on national issues and tried to create a British system of government. Newt is too smart. He knows a lot about European history, and he wants to create a British system of government.

The nationalizers seem to want party government in a fragmented constitutional system, which is no mean feat. This critic contended that Congress is less like Parliament and more like the local school board.

> As members of Congress we like to think of ourselves are junior presidents, when really we are senior county commissioners concerned largely about social security checks, grants for the state arts foundation, and the like. Voters are interested in how issues affect their state. Congressman Mike Synar got in a lot of trouble back home for being quoted in the *New York Times* saying: "I'm not an Oklahoma Congressman, I'm a Congressman from Oklahoma."

House members are neither junior presidents nor senior county commissioners. Rather, they are both: in a system marked by federalism and the separation of powers, they must at once represent national and local perspectives.

Nationalizers sometimes forget Congress' grounding in the politics of competing interests. The institution's parochial bent distinguishes it from the British Parliament. For Congress, local concerns often overrule grand ideas; constituent interests commonly crowd out party principle. Congress' strength is rooted at home, which may be appropriate under the circumstances of the American political culture.

After traveling with numerous members in their districts, Richard Fenno concluded "that any claim by anybody to have a feel for the whole country would be preposterous. For ill or good, no one can comprehend the United States. . . . Only institutionally, not individually, can it be done."[6] More than a century earlier, Tocqueville praised the localism of congressional elections for making lawmakers resistant to "general ideas."[7] This characteristic hampers the sweeping political change sought by policy intellectuals.

For all their emphasis on ideas, critics charge, the nationalizers have placed extraordinary emphasis on the personal faults of Democratic leaders. Some of this criticism has come from within. According to a COS figure:

> I haven't broken with Newt, but I don't favor the personal attacks and the focus on ethics concerns, partly because I think such attacks hurt my friend Newt. It isn't good or useful to be hated in this institution. Newt has invested too much energy on such attacks. . . . I'm not Pollyannaish about politics, but we should be bashing the Democrats about failing to reform welfare rather than the House Bank.

Another Gingrich associate reinforced the point: "I focus on ideas and issues, not personalities. You don't get very far by destroying individuals."

So why does Gingrich, an intellectual who wants to sharpen the debate over ideas, frequently attack Democratic ethics? Gingrich responded: "This is about systemic, institutional corruption, not personality. To ask the Democratic leadership to clean things up would be like asking the old Soviet bureaucracy to reform itself. It ain't going to happen." Gingrich blamed the press for the belief that he personalizes policy differences. What is "most likely to make page one is ethics investigations and personality fights. That is as much a commentary on the news media [as it is on me]." When we pressed Gingrich for a more complete explanation, he said:

> I have a very deep concern about ethics, partly because I come out of the Theodore Roosevelt/LaFollette progressive Republican movement, partly because it's real—I think that corruption is dangerous to every society— and partly because I believe that the minority party has an absolute obligation to take on the majority party when it's corrupt. That's one of our civic duties. It is personalized only to the degree that in fact that's how corruption exists. It's not abstract. It is Jim Wright; it is not in the general theory. And I would say that *Honest Graft* pretty well validated a lot of what I said.

Following a 200-year tradition of reform dating to the Jeffersonians and Anti-Federalists, Gingrich damns the "political class" for abusing government power for selfish and partisan ends. And like Woodrow Wilson, another academic-turned-activist, Gingrich takes offense at the tawdry qualities of Capitol Hill. Using language straight from the academic texts, Gingrich told us of "the nature of dominant systems" and "deviant behavior . . . as measured by the establishment which creates the norms." He said that unions, news media elites, lobbyists, senior bureaucrats, and left-wing activists form "an interlocking and reinforcing mechanism of power analytically."

Coming from a conservative Republican, his analysis sounds surprisingly similar to that of radical sociologist C. Wright Mills: "[T]he people of these higher circles are involved in a set of overlapping 'crowds' and intricately connected 'cliques.' "[8] Indeed, Gingrich could attack the House Democrats' alleged power abuses by quoting another passage from Mills: "The ends of men are often merely hopes, but means are facts within some men's control. That is why all means of power tend to become ends to an elite that is in command of them."[9] Or as Gingrich put it, "a natural establishment does exist."

Gingrich's GOP opponents might contend that talk of "dominant systems" is just a short step from the conspiracy theories that political outsiders have spun ever since the Founding. "Insiders" might argue that Gingrich identifies with the weak tradition in American political thought. According to Herbert Storing, the Anti-Federalists lost the debate over the Constitution not merely because they had less inspiring rhetoric "but because they had the weaker argument."[10] As for their heirs among contemporary outsiders, Ceaser and Busch observe that they run the risk of crossing the line between "a justifiable dissatisfaction with the performance of the political system and an attack on the representational forms that threatens constitutional government itself."[11]

Gingrich and other nationalizers could respond that they seek to strengthen the system by making it more accountable and deliberative. As a point of history, they would deny that theirs is a "weak tradition." In the election of 1800, Gingrich pointed out, "The Jeffersonians just plain beat the Federalists"; indeed the latter party ceased to exist, although their Constitution survived.

The localizers' approach draws on pluralism, the "strong" tradition in American political thought with roots in Madison and the Federalists. A key localizer declared, "I am an incrementalist. I used to be a bombthrower. . . . Rather than go for the long bomb, I'm of the Woody Hayes school: just keep the ball moving." Localizers are more inclined to act than talk, hoping to be responsible and relevant insiders. They will follow the lead of a GOP White House when available. They listen rather than preach. They see the Republican Party's need for a decentralized, inclusive approach.

Their emphasis on local concerns and individual races has a great deal of plausibility, but nationalizers argue that it is woefully inadequate. In a 1983 memo to NRCC, a leading Republican consultant said:

> Yes, a good candidate here, a better campaign there, a critically flawed Democrat someplace else will keep the numbers churning and maybe, though I doubt it, moving up over time—but I don't think that any of us believes, subject to some real watershed event, [our numbers will move up] to anything resembling a stable majority.

Some localizers are too willing to go along to get along, having been raised in the committee system to play the Democrats' game. Others are "fat, dumb, and happy" or simply unprincipled. Such members may see themselves as serving their constituents, which is certainly an honorable part of the job. But it is only *part* of the job. As one member noted, "The problem with Congress is not, as the pundits say, that it's out of touch. The problem is that it is far too *in touch*." Some localizers abet the growth of government and the perpetuation of incumbency for the price of a few appropriations earmarks. Settling for crumbs—or worse, fang marks—only prolongs the House Republicans' minority condition.

Localizers play defense, which is never a winning game for a minority. Many of them stay tied to the ideas of the bureaucratic welfare state, and they ignore the role of new ideas in American politics. They remain "me-too Republicans," merely promoting a little less funding for Democratic policies; their pale moon merely reflects the setting sun of the New Deal Democrats.[12]

Dick Cheney once suggested that there is no single right answer to the strategy question; that the competing perspectives can complement each other. He is not alone. Bob Walker, among others, volunteered a similar argument when asked about the conflicting leadership strategies of Michel and Gingrich:

> . . . they're also complementary. Bob is one who is institutionally oriented, and therefore believes that there are needs to deal in concert with the other side on things that both are important to the country and important to the institution. Newt believes that you ought to always be pressing the other side and forcing them into decisions that they don't want to make, and that there ought to be a constant mood of motion. Those two things in our two leaders are actually helping us, because at

times Bob is letting Newt drive the process forward so that he arrives at the time when he sits down with the other side and they are prepared to do something real, simply because they've been driven into it. At times Newt uses Bob's negotiating strengths to set the base off which we launch the next fight.

In one of the more striking comments we heard in more than 100 interviews, Bill Gavin, long-time aide to the Republican Leader, compared politics to music.

We are told by some that House leadership consists in the virtues of patience, working within the system, negotiating, and getting things done—even if they are not done perfectly. Others say that leadership consists in a scorched-earth policy of confrontation, attacks, and guerilla theater. But in my experience both approaches are needed, simultaneously.

It is like good jazz: In the midst of his improvisatory explorations, a jazz soloist has to be willing to take musical risks because it is in spontaneous risk-taking that great things happen in jazz. But in order to succeed, the risk-taker needs a reliable, steady accompaniment that sets the formal structure within which the creative leap takes place. The underlying chord structure and rock-solid beat provide security and order; the soaring improvisation provides freedom and spontaneity. Combine both and you have the great synergism called art.

The same is true in House politics. The rock-solid political establishmentarian, setting the formal "rules of the game," and the soaring political revolutionary, guided, but not dominated, by the limits, need each other. If the establishment dominates the party, it becomes paralyzed and disintegrates; if the revolutionaries dominate, the party becomes wild and explodes. A great leader uses both elements, without letting either dominate for any length of time.

Three Dimensions of the Puzzle

So what can the House Republicans do? What will make good political jazz? To answer these questions, we move our metaphorical browsing from the music shop back to the toy store, and return to our image of the Rubik's Cube. In this section, we briefly consider individuals, interests, and institutions. In the following section, we offer a more extended discussion of ideas.

Individuals

According to an influential school of thought in social science, it is foolish to appeal to the better angels of individual nature. Political figures are driven only by the rational pursuit of self-interest, this viewpoint contends, and one can change behavior only by manipulating incentives.

We start from a different premise. Of course, interests have enormous significance, so one should never rely only on enlightenment and virtue. One should never neglect them, either. Although proponents of the rational-choice school often cite Madison's analysis of interests, they forget his observations about character. The first aim of any political constitution, he said, should be to obtain rulers "who possess the most wisdom to discern and most virtue to purse the common good of the society."[13]

By this logic, House Republicans should base their leadership choices on a consideration of who can serve their party's common good, and not just the passions of a single wing. Managing House GOP factionalism requires leaders who know how interests affect American politics, who appreciate the needs of different members, yet understand that ideas count. Just as good teachers change their students by getting them to think about new things, and in new ways, legislative leaders can help define a party's principles.[14] As always, context matters. Teachers and leaders alike have to work within a variety of constraints that have a great deal to do with how much they can achieve. But individuals matter, too.

The effective leader of the future will both learn and teach about interest groups that could affect the party's prospects, institutional innovations that could rewrite the rules of the legislative and electoral process, and ideas that could reshape political debate. In 1993, the House Republican leadership dealt with health-care reform in precisely this manner, educating its members in all the dimensions of the issue. Not coincidentally, Newt Gingrich and Dick Armey are both college professors by trade. According to Richard E. Cohen:

> Armey sometimes displays his academic background. In a 14-page memorandum sent to House Republicans in early November, he drew an unflattering parallel between Clinton's health plan and President Carter's unsuccessful energy legislation. . . . His lessons included: "A plan based on faulty premises is inherently defeatable. . . . The side that controls the terms of debate controls the outcome of debate."[15]

A good leader, like a good teacher, must know how to strike a balance between intellectual firmness and tolerance of different points of view. In this respect, moderate Republican Christopher Shays (R-Connecticut) gave Gingrich a compliment that most college professors would like to get: "He is a catalyst. But he is not a dictator."[16]

Interests

What is true of individuals is also true of interests: a legislative party must accommodate a certain degree of pluralism. Gingrich has acknowledged this point:

> [We] have to recognize that we have to get used to fighting ourselves at times and we have to recognize that we are in the business of conflict management. We are not in the business of conflict resolution. You only resolve conflicts by kicking people out and that means you become a minority. So, if you intend to be a majority, you have to be willing to live with a lot of conflict because that is the nature of a majority.[17]

In particular, Republicans have to manage the differences between their traditional economic constituents and religious conservatives. In the 1980s, some of the latter group appeared to have a "rule or ruin" attitude toward the GOP, but more recently they have shown some skill at coalition politics. In the months after President Clinton's election, religious conservatives helped in the successful Senate campaigns of Republicans Paul Coverdell (Georgia) and Kay Bailey Hutchison (Texas) even though both took a pro-choice stand on abortion. Nevertheless, some opponents of the "religious right" seek to purge it from party ranks, arguing that it will eventually extract a steep price for its support. Polling data suggest the perils of this attitude. In 1992, Republican House candidates nationwide got 66 percent of the vote among white born-again or fundamentalist Christians, who made up 17 percent of the electorate.[18] This figure represented the GOP's best showing among any demographic group. If Republicans jettisoned religious conservatives, how would they compensate for the loss of the party's strongest support base?

Republicans must also deal with the politics of ethnicity. In 1993, Republican Mayor Bret Schundler of Jersey City showed that a Republican could indeed win votes from blacks and Latinos. Running for his first full term after a special election the previous fall, Schundler got two-thirds of the vote in a city that is two-thirds minority. One reason for his victory, he said, was simply his willingness to ask blacks and Latinos for their votes, contrary to the conventional wisdom of the First Street consultants who effectively "redline" minority neighborhoods. He also spoke directly to minority voters, not through the "mainline" minority leaders who marched in lockstep against him. His city's voters, he explained, were "tired of the old leadership."[19] Schundler also advanced by embracing innovative policy ideas.

The ethnic politics of the 1990s will pose dilemmas for Republicans. Many Americans believe that the federal government should take strong action to curb immigration, both legal and illegal. At the urging of Pat Buchanan, the 1992 Republican platform pledged to "equip the Border Patrol with the tools, technologies, and structures necessary to secure the border,"[20] a phrase that the Buchanan forces interpreted as an endorsement of a large fence between the United States and Mexico. By taking such stands, Republicans may appeal to the public concern about immigration at the expense of further alienating Latino voters. Similarly a firm stand against racial quotas may appeal to opponents of reverse discrimination, but it could also antagonize black voters. In both instances, it is possible to take positions that are both responsible and responsive: supporting tough security along the border while welcoming lawful immigrants, or opposing quotas while backing affirmative action programs based on economic hardship instead of race. One of the challenges facing party leaders, therefore, is schooling their members in the fine art of principled positioning.

Over one or two election cycles, Republicans cannot completely reverse decades-old voting patterns among minority Americans. They *can* split off enough votes to tip some marginal districts; more important, they can force Democrats to divert valuable campaign resources to seats they thought they would never have to defend.

Institutions

Despite their minority status, House Republicans can still have a small measure of influence over the chamber's rules. Recall from Chapter 4 that they used public and elite opinion to end the secrecy of the discharge petition. Although it is extremely difficult to arouse the public on procedural issues, this case showed that it is possible.

While they lack the numbers to enact campaign finance reforms of their own devising, they can at least fight measures that would make matters worse, particularly bills that would hurt challengers more than incumbents. They can also harness public skepticism about federal spending to cut into the incumbency perquisites and appropriation earmarks that benefit House Democrats.

What about term limits? Congress has never had to operate under term limits, and state legislative term limits are still too recent a phenomenon to yield any hard evidence; accordingly, one can only speculate on this point. As we saw in Chapter 6, Republicans have suffered because they have had a higher retirement rate than Democrats. Over the long run, term limits might diminish this gap. But Democrats have tended to have a "deeper bench" of challengers and open-seat candidates, so unless the GOP strengthens itself at the grass roots, Democrats will be better equipped to take advantage of the more rapid turnover that would accompany term limits. On the other hand, if Newt Gingrich is right about an "interlocking mechanism" that keeps House Democrats in power, tight term limits could help the GOP. Members confined to three two-year terms (the limit endorsed by California voters) would not have much time to cultivate networks of alliance with bureaucrats and interest groups.

We are on firmer ground in discussing relations with the Senate. Although the principle of bicameralism rules out perfect harmony, House Republicans have sought to minimize tensions with Senate Republicans. In 1993, the two groups made some tentative steps to pool their research resources and coordinate their policy messages. One leadership aide said that they had been "working at constructing a very integrated structure."[21] It can never work quite that way, of course, but the very effort could help prevent the intramural conflicts that we saw in Chapter 5.

Ideas

In Chapters 3 and 5, we saw that tax bills have alternately benefited and bedeviled the House Republicans. When they disagree on taxation, they lose. When they unite against higher taxes, they win. In 1993, it seemed that they were once again united. Maintaining such harmony on taxes could greatly help House Republicans in the 1990s, but it would not be *sufficient* to win them a majority. Mere opposition does little to help the GOP: by a two-to-one margin, Americans believed that congressional Republicans opposed the Clinton plan for political reasons, not because they had a realistic alternative.[22]

Republicans blunder when they assume that the record will speak for itself. The voters' perceptions of public policy are influenced by the interpretations they see in the mass media. The Reagan and Bush years brought both good and bad economic news; thanks to writers such as Kevin Phillips, the voters of 1992 looked mainly at the bad. Late in the campaign, recalled White House aide Charles Kolb, the Bush camp recognized that it was "paying the price for having left unchallenged for more than a year the Kevin Phillips view of America."[23] Under Clinton, Republicans cannot challenge the Democratic vision simply by pointing to ongoing economic problems, because voters will blame those troubles more on the GOP than on the Democrats. And it will do them little good to "set the record straight about the Reagan-Bush years," because most voters are bored by statistical debates about economic history. What they need is a vision of the future and a policy argument that reaches beyond the word *no*.

In *The United States of Ambition* Alan Ehrenhalt argues that Republicans suffer from an antigovernment ideology that hampers recruiting and hastens retirements. This situation is a residue of the "sun and moon" arrangement described by Samuel Lubell. From the 1930s to the 1980s, the New Deal largely set the terms of domestic discourse: liberals supported the extension of the New Deal state, while conservatives opposed it. As we saw in Chapter 5, American voters have never completely embraced the conservative side, and some House Republicans despair of changing their minds.

If the 200-proof conservative approach is uninviting, so is "me-too" politics: given a choice between a Democrat and a pseudo-Democrat, voters will tend to pick the genuine article. Even worse, fueling the growth of the federal government only encourages bureaucratic careerism and pork-barrel politics.

Former White House aide James Pinkerton has described another approach, which he calls "The New Paradigm." Although the term itself would not have much appeal on the campaign trail, it comprises ideas that may: replacing bureaucracies with markets; expanding the choices available to citizens and consumers; empowering the disadvantaged to take part in the market economy; decentralizing government; and appraising policies by their accomplishments instead of their intentions. Specific examples of "New Paradigm" policies include school choice, tenant management of public housing, health-care vouchers, and privatization of public services. There are several reasons why House Republicans might want to build their domestic policy proposals around "New Paradigm" concepts.

First, these policies potentially have appeal because they serve the popular *ends* of the welfare state without resorting to its increasingly discredited *means*. Despite the nostalgic wishes of those who would simply repeal the New Deal, Americans believe that government should address problems such as poverty and inadequate health care. Americans favor limited government, but effective government.

Second, most Republicans can embrace the New Paradigm because it squares with the traditional GOP beliefs in free enterprise and local government. Some on the "old right" deride it as "big-government conservatism," but theirs is a minority position within the party. After all, a reinvigorated federalism was central to the domestic policies of Ronald Reagan.

Third, though the New Paradigm is not a vaporous set of platitudes, neither is it a rigid and detailed dogma. On a number of issues, it can accommodate a range of opinions. For instance, two of the most prominent "New Paradigm" Republicans of the 1990s are the prolife Jack Kemp and the prochoice William Weld, the governor of Massachusetts. Although Pinkerton tends toward the libertarian side of social issues, some of his New Paradigm themes have been picked up by the executive director of the Christian Coalition, who sees them as a way of strengthening family life.[24]

Fourth, the New Paradigm has built a promising record at the ballot box. As mentioned earlier, Mayor Bret Schundler triumphed in a traditionally Democratic city by campaigning on these ideas. In Wisconsin, another Democratic stronghold, Governor Tommy Thompson has used New Paradigm ideas on welfare reform and other issues to revive the state GOP. In 1993, for the first time in twenty-eight years, Republicans won control of the Wisconsin Senate. This victory is particularly significant, since Ehrenhalt singled out the Wisconsin legislature as an example of entrenched Democratic control.

Big ideas can nurture the grass roots. The realignment of the 1930s changed voting patterns in presidential elections, yet for years the Democratic hold on lower offices remained much more tenuous. Meanwhile, FDR and his New Deal inspired a new generation of Democrats to get involved in politics. During the 1940s and 1950s, this new generation took over and strengthened local party organizations. Unlike the old-line patronage Democrats that they displaced, they had a zest for ideas that made them attractive to a wide variety of voters, and they started to win elections in areas that had once seemed forever Republican. This second stage of the New Deal realignment culminated in the congressional elections of 1958, where a smashing Democratic victory dealt the House Republicans a blow from which they have still not recovered.[25]

The New Paradigm is not an all-encompassing governing philosophy, but it can provide a positive vision of what a limited and effective government can do. Republicans need such a vision. According to Vin Weber: "Our major mistake has been to focus on *wedge* issues against the Democrats without also creating *magnet* issues that would attract the public. Both wedge and magnet issues are essential, but because we concentrated on the first while ignoring the second, we acquired a reputation as primarily negative and confrontational."[26] An effort to build magnet issues would be consistent with GOP tradition. Lincoln said that "in all that people can do for themselves in their separate capacities, government ought not to interfere," but he also supported the Homestead Act and other measures that amounted to what historians have called "a capitalist revolution."[27]

The New Paradigm is not a silver bullet. No set of policy ideas alone can solve all of the GOP's problems at the level of individuals, interests, and institutions. Moreover, the New Paradigm is not the exclusive domain of the GOP. During his first year in office, President Clinton announced a number of initiatives that seemed consistent with the concept, at least on the rhetorical level. So as House Republicans develop their own philosophy, they face the additional task of convincing the public that the Democratic version is a bad imitation.

Ideas are more than mere political weapons. Party leaders must take them seriously, for their policy implications as well as their political impact. Decentralization, for instance, is not a mere euphemism for cutbacks but a well-rooted approach to domestic problems. At the 1992 Republican convention, Ronald Reagan challenged Americans "to invigorate democracy in your own neighborhoods."[28] Such language echoes Tocqueville's praise for America's administrative decentralization. Tocqueville made clear that centralized bureaucracies strangle the voluntary associations needed for self-government.[29] These organizations—churches, charities, civic groups—help remedy the alienation of modern society by teaching citizens about their rights and responsibilities, and educating them in the "art of associating." Such mediating structures form our character as citizens capable of self-government.[30] To Tocqueville, man's most natural right, "after that of acting on his own, is that of combining his efforts with those of his fellows and acting together. Therefore the right of association seems to me by nature almost as inalienable as individual liberty."[31]

The New Paradigm seeks to limit government not as an end in

itself, but as a way of empowering individuals and strengthening communities. Tocqueville criticized those among his contemporaries who claimed "that as citizens become weaker and more helpless, the government must become proportionately more skillful and active, so that society should do what is no longer possible for individuals."[32] Bureaucratic solutions may backfire: "The more government takes the place of associations, the more will individuals lose the idea of forming associations and need the government to come to their help. This is a vicious circle of cause and effect."[33] The danger is great: "The morals and intelligence of a democratic people would be in as much danger as its commerce and industry if ever a government wholly usurped the place of private associations. Feelings and ideas are renewed, the heart enlarged, and the understanding developed only by the reciprocal action of men one upon another."[34]

In this light, Republicans' opposition to new taxes and bureaucracies has a positive purpose and cannot be reduced to mindless opposition to government. Consequently, GOP disarray on the issue of taxes could overwhelm Republican messages on other issues. The late Lee Atwater, a student of Sun Tzu and other military thinkers, said that the GOP could gain ground by supporting "quality" government that would help more and intrude less. But he emphasized that the party had to maintain its "fortress" on the tax issue.

Conclusion

Even if the GOP does everything right on the four dimensions just described, it may still fall short of a majority. If this book has demonstrated anything, it is that the House Republicans are not entirely masters of their fate.

Yet they can improve their chances, provided they stop being their own worst enemy. One important reason why House Republicans are a minority is that they cannot agree on the causes and cures of their minority status; they spend precious time and energy fighting among themselves and with other Republicans over how to become a majority. They need to see how the pieces of the puzzle fit together; they need to understand the connections of interests, institutions, individuals, and ideas.

The ideal House Republicans would appreciate the grounding of the legislative process in a pluralism of interests; they would understand the institutional constraints on action and ideas; they would empathize with their colleagues' electoral predicaments; and they would be aware of the power of ideas and attuned to the necessary balance of a governing philosophy.

House Republicans have to master the art of political jazz. With practice, they can ready themselves for that day when conditions line up just right and they can sound the notes that will bring down the Democratic Jericho.

Notes

1. Richard F. Fenno, Jr., *Watching Politicians: Essays on Participant Observation* (Berkeley: IGS Press, 1990), 100.
2. Quoted in Dan Balz, "Frustrations Embitter House GOP," *Washington Post*, April 29, 1985, A4.
3. We are indebted to Michael Malbin for this insight.
4. Quoted in Richard E. Cohen, "On the Edge," *National Journal*, December 4, 1993, 2888.
5. Charles Fenyvesi, "Washington Whispers," *U.S. News and World Report*, August 16, 1993, 20.
6. Fenno, *Watching Politicians*, 93.
7. Alexis de Tocqueville, *Democracy in America*, trans. George Lawrence, ed. J. P. Mayer (Garden City, N.Y.: Doubleday/Anchor Books, 1969), 441–442.
8. C. Wright Mills, *The Power Elite* (New York: Oxford University Press/Galaxy Books, 1959), 11.
9. Ibid., 23.
10. Herbert J. Storing, *What the Anti-Federalists Were For* (Chicago: University of Chicago Press, 1981), 71.
11. James Ceaser and Andrew Busch, *Upside Down and Inside Out: The 1992 Elections and American Politics* (Lanham, Md.: Rowman and Littlefield/Littlefield Adams Quality Paperbacks, 1993), 26.
12. Samuel Lubell, *The Future of American Politics*, 2d ed. (Garden City, N.Y.: Doubleday/Anchor Books, 1956), 214–15.
13. *The Federalist*, ed. Jacob E. Cooke (1961; reprint, Middletown, Conn.: Wesleyan University Press, 1982), number 57, p. 384. See also James Q. Wilson, "Interests and Deliberation in the American Republic, or, Why James Madison Would Never Have Received the James Madison Award," *PS: Political Science and Politics* 23 (December 1990): 558–62.
14. William K. Muir, Jr., compares a legislature to a school in *Legislature: California's School for Politics* (Chicago: University of Chicago Press, 1982). In a little-noticed 1981 article, Gingrich explained that the decentralization of society called for a new kind of lawmaker: "a student-teacher who works and educates to solve the nation's problems." Newt Gingrich and Marianne

Gingrich, "Post-Industrial Politics: The Leader as Learner," *The Futurist*, December 1981, 29.

15. Cohen, "On the Edge," 2891.

16. Ibid., 2889.

17. Newt Gingrich, address to Southern Republican Leadership Conference, Raleigh, North Carolina, March 30, 1990.

18. Voter Research and Surveys release, general election, November 3, 1992.

19. Grover G. Norquist, "Rainbow Republican," *American Spectator*, September 1993, 57–58.

20. Republican National Convention, *The Vision Shared: Uniting Our Family, Our Country, Our World* (Houston: Republican National Convention, 1992), 37.

21. Susan B. Glasser, "Hill Republicans Struggle to Fill 'Research Gap' Resulting From Loss of White House," *Roll Call*, January 18, 1993, 8, 60.

22. Charles Cook, "GOP Can't Count on Clinton's Woes to Bring '94 Success," *Roll Call*, May 10, 1993, 9.

23. Charles Kolb, *White House Daze: The Unmaking of Domestic Policy in the Bush Years* (New York: Free Press, 1994), 283.

24. Ralph Reed, Jr., "Casting a Wider Net," *Policy Review* 65 (Summer 1993): 31–35.

25. James L. Sundquist, *Dynamics of the Party System: Alignment and Realignment of Political Parties in the United States*, rev. ed. (Washington, D.C.: Brookings, 1983), 262–66.

26. Quoted in Adam Meyerson, "Wedges and Magnets: Vin Weber on Conservative Opportunities," *Policy Review* 52 (Spring 1990): 42.

27. James M. McPherson, *Abraham Lincoln and the Second American Revolution* (New York: Oxford University Press, 1990), 40.

28. "Reagan Tells Audience, Country: 'We Need George Bush,' " *Congressional Quarterly Weekly Report*, August 22, 1992, 2546.

29. William A. Schambra, "The Quest for Community, and the Quest for a New Public Philosophy" (paper prepared for presentation at the American Enterprise Institute's Public Policy Week, December 5–8, 1993). See also Schambra, "Turf Battles: The Parties Clash Over Community," *Public Opinion*, July/August 1988, 17–19, 60.

30. Robert A. Nisbet, *The Quest for Community* (New York: Oxford University Press, 1970); Peter L. Berger and Richard John Neuhaus, *To Empower People: The Role of Mediating Structures in Public Policy* (Washington, D.C.: American Enterprise Institute, 1977).

31. Tocqueville, *Democracy in America*, 193.

32. Ibid., 515.

33. Ibid., 515.

34. Ibid., 515.

Index

175

About the Authors

William F. Connelly, Jr., is Associate Professor of Politics at Washington and Lee University in Lexington, Virginia. He has a Ph.D. in American government from the University of Virginia and an M.A. in political science from Boston College. He has worked as an American Political Science Association Congressional Fellow for former Congressman Dick Cheney and Senator Richard G. Lugar.

John J. Pitney, Jr., is Assistant Professor of Government at Claremont McKenna College in Claremont, California. He has a Ph.D. in political science from Yale. He has worked as an American Political Science Association Congressional Fellow for Senator Alfonse D'Amato and former Congressman Dick Cheney. He has also worked on the staffs of the House Republican Research Committee and the Republican National Committee.